Beethoven's Symphonies

Unlocking the Masters Series, No. 14

Beethoven's Symphonies

A Guided Tour

John Bell Young

AMADEUS
PRESS

An Imprint of Hal Leonard Corporation
New York

Published in 2008 by Amadeus Press
An Imprint of Hal Leonard Corporation
7777 West Bluemound Road
Milwaukee, WI 53213

Trade Book Division Editorial Offices
19 West 21st Street, New York, NY 10010

Printed in the United States of America

Book design by Snow Creative Services

Library of Congress Cataloging-in-Publication Data is available upon request.

ISBN: 978-1-57467-169-8

www.amadeuspress.com

For my mother

Dorothy Burgess Young (1919–2007)

Contents

Acknowledgments   ix

Introduction   xiii

Chapter 1. Intonatsiia, or the Art of Listening   1

Chapter 2. Context and Significance   11

Chapter 3. Symphony No. 1 in C Major, Op. 21   17

Chapter 4. Symphony No. 2 in D Major, Op. 36   33

Chapter 5. Symphony No. 3 in E-flat Major, Op. 55 ("Eroica")   43

Chapter 6. Symphony No. 4 in B-flat Major, Op. 60   55

Chapter 7. Symphony No. 5 in C Minor, Op. 67   63

Chapter 8. Symphony No. 6 in F Major, Op. 68 ("Pastoral")   81

Chapter 9. Symphony No. 7 in A Major, Op. 92   93

Chapter 10. Symphony No. 8 in F Major, Op. 93   101

Chapter 11. Symphony No. 9 in D Minor, Op. 125   107

Glossary   121

Selected Bibliography   129

CD Track Listing   131

Acknowledgments

Writing about music is no easy task. One is easily persuaded by force of habit as much as long-held beliefs in the veracity of a point of view, as if objectivity were the only thing that mattered.

But as any musician worth his salt knows only too well, music is so complex and abundant as to invite any number of perspectives. And where those perspectives are as informed as they are imaginative, they are worthy of contemplation.

Much the same can be said of any artistic endeavor, and writing is no exception. I am indebted to a number of friends and colleagues for their assistance and advice, several of whom did not live to see the completion of this project nor were even aware that what I learned from them would contribute to it so substantially.

Above all there is my late mother, Dorothy Burgess Young, without whose support and unflinching belief in my abilities I could never have written this volume, or even so much as played a single note at the piano. Whether eerie coincidence or something born of a grander scheme, Amadeus Press offered me the formidable challenge of writing a dozen books for its distinguished roster only thirty minutes after my mother's passing in July 2007 at age eighty-eight. And so it is in honor of her that I commit to this, the first of these tomes, and to the others to come.

There are in addition a number of individuals whom I would like to thank for their support and advice, literary and otherwise, while writing this book. My thanks to Joseph Early and Sandra Rush, whose infinite patience, innumerable kindnesses, critical overview, and thoughtful consideration were not only proof of the deepest friendship, but equal to the best editorial advice; to Reni Santoni and Tracy Newman, without whose assistance and counsel at a time when I most needed it I would surely never have been able to complete these works; to my best friend and partner, Michael Vincent Connolly, for his friendship, solidarity, and unwavering faith in my abilities and perseverance; to Michael York, Hugh Downs, and Eric Le Van, all experienced authors who showed tremendous patience in reading the manuscript and commenting on its efficacy; to my neighbors Mark and Camilla Tarmy, whose understanding and generosity of spirit know no bounds and who have patiently put up with my sometimes impossible demands for convenience and quietude; to Margarita Fyodorova, who taught me all about intonation and much more; to Rick Bechard, whose eye and ear as a documentary filmmaker were invaluable, as he helped me to reconsider both style and narrative, which I can only hope find in these volumes a writer who does them justice; to Gordon and Emily Jones, Joseph Fichter, Julie Marsden, Greg Brown, and others in the extended Putney School family, for their encouragement, kindness, and help; to John Cerullo, the publisher of Amadeus Press, for his goodwill was an extraordinary demonstration of courage, in that he invested his faith and his corporate resources in this longtime columnist and critic but untested book author; and to the exemplary editorial staff at Amadeus Press, including my meticulous copy editor Angela Buckley and project editor Jessica Burr.

Finally, to those who are no longer with us, I extend my gratitude in ways that I can only hope will be borne aloft on the wings of angels. From these individuals I learned much of what I know of music. Among them are Constance Keene, a great pianist who was my teacher and mentor for nearly thirty years; Michel Block, likewise among the great pianists of the twentieth century, whose extraordinary musical savoir faire, supported by his personal gentility, provided a continual source of knowledge and enrichment; James Landrum Fessenden, a brilliant philosopher and musician whose premature death was a blow to all who knew him, and whose authority in any number of disciplines from aesthetics to epistemology and psychoanalysis has always proven invaluable; and to both Claudio Arrau and Ernst Levy, each of whom taught me more about Beethoven and music making, in my few brief encounters with them, than most could have done in a lifetime.

Finally, my thanks to Dover Publications, whose exquisitely printed and always reliable editions of the Beethoven symphonies, in full score and in Liszt transcriptions for piano, made my labors that much easier; and to Fred Maroth of Music & Arts Records, who provided the magnificent recordings of Wilhelm Furtwängler that accompany this book.

Introduction

Of all the figures in the history of Western music, few have been exploited, extolled, sanctified, and mythologized as thoroughly as Ludwig van Beethoven. For more than two centuries, the popular myths surrounding him have taken on a life of their own. Who would not be hard-pressed to think of a single biography or analytical thesis, which by now number in the thousands, that has failed to paint this great man as a surly, antisocial, and incorruptible misanthrope? How often has Beethoven, whose music ignited political philosophy as much as it inspired independence, been sold wholesale as a pugnacious, belligerent brute with a heart of gold and an ethereal spirit that made his personal shortcomings wholly forgivable?

Beethoven's transformation from a human being into a cultural icon and the spiritual embodiment of humanity itself was hardly something that took place postmortem. The magnification of his persona began to take root in his lifetime, as early as 1800 with the debut of his First Symphony. Even in the absence of electronic technology and mass communication, Beethoven's celebrity was assured. Whether his fame was exclusively a consequence of his musical output, or tied to his popular image as a complex, combative, and immodest individual, remains to be seen and probably doesn't matter. What does matter is that his music, from the outset, did more than impress his intellectual contemporaries: it spoke to everyone, to experts and laypersons alike, and continues to do so nearly two centuries after his death.

It would be naive and perhaps disingenuous to attribute the enormous fame he achieved in a world free of mass media as a fluke, or solely as the result of his unique musical voice. On the contrary, while he was determined, like any other composer, to have his music widely published, performed, and understood, he was nothing if not shrewd in his professional judgment. Beethoven knew perfectly well who and what he was.

Though obliged to compete with his colleagues for recognition, he also straddled a delicate balance between blind obedience to his wealthy benefactors, on the one hand, and taking care to avoid alienating the public, on the other. His resolve to defend his Republican idealism was in itself a form of promotional, albeit intuitive, savoir faire. To have defied authority in the manner he so often did—what we would describe today as "talking back to power"—put him at risk in a politically volatile and ever-so-autocratic Europe. While his colleagues kowtowed to royalty, Beethoven refused to so much as remove his hat, as was the custom, as they passed by. A weaker man, to say nothing of a less gifted artist, would have been destroyed if not imprisoned for daring to challenge the status quo (much less the ubiquitous secret police who scoured Vienna undercover in those days) as he often did in public and in private, no matter his métier.

But Beethoven knew well the power of contradiction and the advantages of cultivating controversy. In this context, his music would not only thrive, but also stimulate the public's imagination to an extraordinary degree. In music at once powerful and intimate, defiant and thoughtful, he gave voice to the common man. He posed a threat to a crumbling political culture that embraced the idea that any society, if it is to be tamed, must be divided and *then* conquered.

The French Revolution of 1789 was still fresh in everyone's mind, not least among members of the ruling class, who did not wish to see themselves end up like Marie Antoinette. Music, which by 1800 had evolved from a passive entertainment for the well-heeled to an object of philosophical contemplation for all who had ears, had the power to motivate large numbers of people. Beethoven's musical language was ripe with musical gestures that could be interpreted as symbolic: of freedom, of defiance, of revolution. In this context, the symphony assumed special significance, becoming by the turn of the nineteenth century an emblem of community spirit and cooperation.

Whether such an interpretation is based on anything musically concrete remains to be seen. Certainly, the issue has been a subject for debate for more than a century, beginning with Eduard Hanslick in the 1850s and culminating in the twentieth century in the theoretical critiques of Hans Pfitzner, Paul Bekker, Theodor W. Adorno, and Heinrich Schenker. Absolutists such as Hanslick, Schenker, and Pfitzner, champions of the idea of the autonomy of a musical composition, held that meaning is revealed only by a work's immanent content. The anti-absolutists, such as Bekker, countered with the argument that symbolic, extramusical determinants, such as a composer's political ideology or poetic ideals, were no less important and equally responsible for communicating, to any listener, its substance. This debate, which today is perhaps less relevant than it was a hundred years ago, has now become fodder for musical semiotics, an offspring of linguistics that combines reception theory (how we react to music) with structural analysis.

Indeed, the notion that Beethoven's music was in itself revolutionary, that is, a by-product of the political thinking that swept Europe off its feet in the late eighteenth century, is as misleading as it is overbroad. While it is true that the French Revolution inspired change in every area of society—in politics and the arts, science and religion, literature and technology—it would be inopportune to merely presume cause and effect, as if Beethoven had willy-nilly decided to codify "revolution," a broad enough concept in its own right, in musical categories. On the contrary, he availed himself of all the extant tools and laws of composition, reinventing them to some degree. Indeed, just as French Revolution inspired the world to renew its faith in the potential of the individual and the power of collective cooperation, so Beethoven invested his powers in expanding the potential of musical form and content.

But one thing is certain: Beethoven saw nothing worthwhile about ignoring the everyday struggles of the poor and working classes in favor of kowtowing to the decadent demands of the aristocracy. The momentous upheaval in social, economic, and political spheres brought about by the French Revolution extended to all areas of socialized behavior, including the arts and sciences; everyone began thinking outside of the box, as it were, in an effort to reinvent the world in the spirit of fraternity and collaboration. Beethoven's ability to grasp and even exploit the direction in which his changing social environment was moving was as much a part of his genius as his musical probity, though the extent to which his tastes in extramusical arenas affected his musical disposition was more relevant to the time in which he lived than it was to his composing.

Even so, it is hardly a stretch to argue, no matter how glibly, that the art of any age reflects its anxieties and frustrations as much as its joys and expectations. Beethoven's music certainly did that, and it reflected, too, a new movement in literature and philosophy that took pains to distinguish the beautiful (an idea that had traditionally extolled pleasure and the superficial and was given over to the purely representative) from the sublime. From this new perspective and in contradiction to the notion of beauty, the sublime was a concept of the universal, one that sought to reconcile the finite with the infinite as it recognized the legitimacy, in artistic representation, of opposing ideas and emotions, not the least of which were pleasure and pain, beauty and terror. Whereas the concept of beauty naively relied on decorum, innocence, and instant gratification—the principal postulates of its aesthetics—the sublime embraced critical thinking, historical process, and the synthesis of contradictory and antagonistic forces. Now elevated to philosophy, music was liberated from its earlier dependence, through representational means, on speech. Unlike language, music could postulate nothing but mean everything. And yet it was precisely this ambiguity that the new thinking both welcomed and exploited.

In his symphonies, which fulfilled the promise of a form now canonized by this new thinking-man's society, Beethoven pushed the boundaries of musical experience. Emotional satisfaction and even the passage of time itself became a new kind of artistic experience. Emboldened, asynchronous rhythms, unexpected accentuations, jarring dissonances, and the prolongation of harmonic fields as a means of creating musical tension all had the effect of compressing time, vortex-like. The sheer volume of compositional information he proffers in any one of his symphonies is staggering; in offering so much data in a relatively short span, Beethoven demands a great deal from the listener.

Yet it is precisely by these means that he challenged restraint, the very principle of classical decorum. He exploded his listeners' expectations with music that could erupt suddenly and violently as readily as it could assuage and console. It was music that, whether a matter of deliberation on its composer's part or not, gave voice to the sublime.

To say that his music was radical, however, is merely a truism, as that radicalism was hardly born in a vacuum. Like other composers of the day—Dussek, Hummel, Spohr, and Weber among them—he owed an enormous debt to Haydn and Mozart, who likewise had changed and emboldened music thirty years before Beethoven became a household name in Europe. What distinguished him from the legion of musical mediocrities that populated late eighteenth-century Europe was the ingenious innovation he brought to *existing* musical forms. This he did in a way that was so exquisitely detailed and unapologetic—and thus risky—as to put his more status-minded colleagues to shame.

While he was hardly immune to the commercial dimensions of sustaining a career, he did so pretty much on his own terms, and without resorting, at least as often as other composers, to writing light or programmatic music (with the exception of his so-called Battle Symphony, folk song settings, and several other minor works). Shrewder still was his manipulation of the patrons who sponsored him; while he did what he could to assuage them and lobby their interest in his music, he was aware, too, that this was not enough. To the leading musicians of his day, even those who expressed their disdain for him at court or in public, his music was sufficiently fascinating to compel them to recommend him to their employers, namely, the aristocracy. Even the least talented among his colleagues could plainly see that Beethoven was a rising star, so why not hold on to his coattails on the way up?

There was a heightened perception in the early nineteenth century that something was coming to an end, namely, exclusivity of access to art. Art music had largely been the province of the upper classes, who paid for its creation and performance in their own homes. But as the overwhelming prestige of opera in comparison to instrumental music began to fade, symphonic music came to be viewed as the embodiment of cooperation, brotherhood, and community. Music became something purposeful, a means to inspire a synthesis between the individual and the collective, and thus served as a model of organization, in an ideal world, for the state. In short, music became a paradigm for social interaction.

With his new symphonic creations espousing musical ideas as bold as they were optimistic, Beethoven effectively extinguished the notion of difference between aristocrat and commoner. Everyone was welcome to participate in the experience of his musical ideology. For those who might consider that statement to be an exaggeration, there is no doubt that at the very least he endorsed the idea of solidarity and egalitarianism and welcomed the public perception of his work as being akin to those ideals. That perception has survived him by two centuries.

In spite of their essential conformity to the aesthetics and compositional laws of the classical canon, Beethoven's symphonies became, for many, the embodiment of victory in the face of adversity. The idea of "overcoming" through personal and collective struggle was both the political and aesthetic rallying cry of the day. Thus it is no wonder these symphonies were so readily embraced by popular culture, as Beethoven was himself transformed by it into a symbol of defiance and freedom. In contradiction to the unctuous bowing to authority that his colleagues settled for in hope of finding or simply maintaining a court appointment, he embraced controversy, not so much by exploiting or shunning it as by living it. In Napoleonic Europe, Beethoven not only stood on principle, he stood *for* principle.

If the current volume has any purpose, it is to pay homage to the spirit of early nineteenth-century idealism and to explore ways to enhance musical experience. Notwithstanding E. T. A. Hoffmann's celebrated critique of the Fifth Symphony, which laid blame on poorly trained listeners, no one should have to be an authority on music history or on compositional or performance techniques to be personally fulfilled by a great work of music. While that in no way dismisses the value of knowledge aforethought and experience, the fact remains that the power and meaning of music are broad. Music has different meanings for different people. Whereas in one individual it may evoke a memory or an image that can be viewed as purely associative, in another the contemplation and analysis of its many parts may lead toward nirvana. Whatever the case, what matters in the end is the work itself and its ability to enrich our lives as individuals and as a society.

It may be that, in the current social climate, the humanitarian dimensions of great music have been abandoned in favor of a kind of listening that relegates one famous masterpiece after another to background noise. It's too easy to blame pop music, whose ubiquity, arising from its musical simplicity and from contemporary mechanisms of commercial distribution and promotion, has so totally captured the popular imagination. Rather than attempt to utter dictums and lecture anyone on the validity of any musical genre, or the relative value of complexity in art, the best idea remains as French as the 1789 Revolution, to wit, *chacun à son goût.*

In this and future volumes for Amadeus Press, it is my objective to survey great music from a personal perspective, just as anyone would. Whatever I can convey of my ideas about listening, though informed by analytical scrutiny and historical data, will not be enslaved by technical analysis. While academia continues to do its job in the classroom, pointing out the idiosyncratic formalities of this or that composition as it teaches students to more effectively recognize compositional strategies, I prefer to do what I can to bring music to life in a kind of dialectical dance. These slim volumes for Amadeus Press, then, are part musical analysis and part interpretation, but above all a personal appreciation. My work here is not intended to be nor should it be construed as a work of scholarship.

Nowhere will I presume that the reader will be following my musical observations, or the accompanying CD, with a score in hand. So often when we listen to music, things seem to fly off the page of the score, or from the hands of the performer, in ways that strike us as inexplicably new and exciting, as if we had just heard the piece for the first time. Perhaps that's just how it should be. In any case, in attempting to put myself in the shoes of listeners, both those who are familiar with this music and those who may not be, I will do my best to bring them into the dynamic fold of the music as it reveals itself. And while there are certainly advantages to examining the score, there is also much to be said for letting your ears do what they do best when you trust your instincts: listening!

Music is an adventure. If I am successful in cultivating in readers a renewed curiosity about its many recesses and shadows, rivulets and canyons, all the better. Certainly I make no claims to be right or wrong; after all, the most rigorous harmonic and formal analyses are probably better served by theorists and scholars whose work is more useful to each other than it is to nonexpert music lovers. The latter are those who simply strive to become as intimate with music as they can without becoming scientists. It is to those *amateurs de la musique* that I dedicate this volume, and I hope they will find within its pages something of value.

—John Bell Young
Putney, Vermont, 2007

Intonatsiia, or the Art of Listening

If there is one compelling issue that governs our relationship to music, it's the act of listening. Given the complexity and sophistication of most "classical music," passive listening is inadequate. To get the most out of the musical experience of listening, something more is needed.

In *Unlocking the Masters*, we will provide ideas and even some concrete tips for music lovers to enhance their listening experience. This is why, before embarking on an exploration of the music this book has to offer, I'd like to introduce a singularly valuable concept cultivated and named by Russian musical culture. It's called *intonatsiia*.

Intonatsiia translates into English as "intonation," which in more generic households can be construed to mean whether or not an instrument is playing in tune. In Russia, *intonatsiia* refers not only to intonation as we know it, but to musical expression. Therefore, I prefer to use the Russian word to help us think beyond intonation as we commonly know it. And for Russians, who learn the value of intonatsiia as children, it is so universally understood and accepted that no one even bothers to talk about it anymore. It's something one learns as easily and with no less assurance as riding a bicycle. It's a skill that, once learned, is learned for life.

So just what is intonatsiia? Essentially, it is the codification of the musical tension that governs intervallic relations (distance between two pitches); it refers to dynamic tension, engendered by harmony and rhythm that occurs *between* the notes. This concept proposes an aesthetic connection between musical expression and speech. The aim of intonatsiia, as a tool of listening and performance, is to sculpt a musical gesture as it assimilates inflection. From this perspective, it is an interpretive device that allows a musician to illuminate the psychological dimensions of a composition and for listeners to experience this.

The fundamental breeding ground of intonatsiia is the *interval*, that is, the distance between two pitches. Intonatsiia, then, refers to the attraction that one tone has for another. We call the nature or character of that attraction *affect*.

When two or more pitches are sequentially distributed, they form independent, identifiable rhythmic units, or *motives*. Motivic material articulates a work, informs its immanent character and lends it consistency as it progresses. Motives are, in effect, the musical motors of a composition that drive it on. Angst, longing, tension, resolution of tension, anger, frustration, contentment, and so on somehow hemorrhage into music and find symbolic expression in compositional categories. In the rhythmic play of these tiny compositional motors lurks the source of all musical declamation: here music whispers, cajoles, rages, sighs, ponders, shouts, seduces.

This idea, which blossomed in the nineteenth century and came of age in the twentieth, has proved a rich subject for aesthetic contemplation. Take Mussorgsky, for example, a late nineteenth-century populist Russian composer; in an effort to articulate the concerns and psychology of everyday life, he saw an opportunity to create something more than glib program music. But a half-century earlier, Beethoven, whose works both developed and indicted compositional conventions and thus the status quo, likewise exploited the symbolic potential of music.

Of course, there is a great deal of room for interpretation in all this. What any individual musical work may "mean" is inherently ambiguous, and it is precisely that ambiguity that fascinated artists and philosophers alike at the dawn of the nineteenth century. The age of reason had given way to the age of fantasy. This development was in itself significant, because up until then, purely instrumental music was considered inferior to music with words, not the least of which was opera. At last musicians and the public began to see that maybe, just maybe, the violent sforzandos, dramatic pauses, and other dynamic devices introduced by Beethoven had something to say in their own right. What that was exactly remained to be seen, absent a lexicon or vocabulary that, like words, specifically defined what this or that musical gesture was supposed to indicate. This left the door wide open for musical symbolism, where suggestion and innuendo held court. The age of romanticism had arrived.

So what concerns intonatsiia, then, are not the notes themselves, but what occurs *between* them, and the degree of musical tension this "betweenness" signifies in their given context. Intonatsiia presides in the realm of intuition and bridges the gap between music and language, between artistic expression and social conventions. Intervallic space is rarely empty, but a kind of gravitational field where tones emerge, shift, migrate, collide, and resurface. Each pitch, from this perspective, becomes a point of condensation that absorbs rhythmic energy. Each note becomes "pregnant" with the one that follows. Working much like neurons in a brain, intonatsiia duplicates those sinuous structures; it is a synaptic process that telegraphs meaning across distance. Thus, once purged of words, which in speech and song play host to intonatsiia, instrumental music is free to give sanctuary to pure affect and inflection.

It should be noted that silence (rests) and distance, while properties of intonatsiia, are not identical to it. On the contrary, they are a measure of its inflective character and its affective potential. You might say that intonatsiia is to music what light and shadows are to painting: a means for determining perspective.

What occurs between notes, between phrases, and also between entire movements is dynamic, alive, and prescient. Musical space (by this I refer not only to rests or silence, but to the distention in time of a pitch or group of pitches as it expands outward, sometimes in stasis) is filled with expectation, pregnant with what is to come and redolent of what has just occurred. The compelling inevitability we experience when a simple seventh chord resolves onto the tonic, for example, or when a tritone (an interval consisting of three consecutive whole tones; F-natural to B-natural, for example) moves outward to a minor sixth (or inward to major third) is something we experience viscerally, even physically, in the gut, as it were.

The concept of intonatsiia requires the listener to develop the ability to *imagine* and to feel the progressive dynamics of a musical work with visceral intensity. In other words, we strive to relate to the life *between* the notes, and not merely to their vibratory properties the moment they are produced. "We create the necessary continuity that does not actually take place," opines Charles Rosen, who likewise credits the listener's imagination as responsible for filling in the gaps. In his view, "the expressive force of the music causes us to imagine as actually existing what is only implied."

In America, the art of intonatsiia has largely been unexplored by the listening public, who would most definitely benefit from familiarity with its principles. From childhood we are not so much taught to listen as trained to hear. There's a big difference, as the former concerns engaged understanding, while the latter assumes a posture of passive indifference. A large sector of the music-loving public is simply untrained in the context of *listening*. The good news is that it is not at all difficult to become an engaged listener; like any other skill, listening can be learned and cultivated. You might think of listening as a kind of muscle; with regular exercise it will become very resilient indeed. A specific means of expression—that is, a way of turning a phrase into something vibrant, plastic, and flexible, or a motive into something shapely, rhythmically articulate, and easily identifiable—can certainly be conveyed and taught with precision to any burgeoning musician. But average listeners, too, no matter their musical background, can likewise learn not only to recognize these events, but to distinguish their efficacy in any given performance.

Doubtless, some of you are familiar with the frustration of hearing students as well as professional performers who play flatly, without expression, as if the musical terrain were the cornfields of Iowa or the Dutch lowlands; there are no hills and valleys, no recesses and shadows, no mountains and vistas. Such performances fail to move us, because they are like one big canvas where every note and every phrase is played with equal importance. They demonstrate little if any feel for harmonic orientation, nor for the immanent tension and internecine dramas that fuel the work at hand. Absent, too, is any sense of movement toward concrete compositional goals, as if musical space were devoid of compositional *events*.

Intonatsiia cultivates an awareness of such events. From this perspective, each interval assumes its own character; as a general rule (but one that is hardly written in stone), the larger the interval, the longer the time should be taken to move across it. More often than not that extra time can be measured in milliseconds; by no means does this suggest that note values should be radically altered or distorted. We are talking, after all, about *nuance*. Nikolaus Harnoncourt refers to these affective fluctuations as *microdynamics*, which in turn rely on musicians' ability to deftly characterize and shape even the smallest motivic units. And as they do so, we as listeners invest our own imaginative powers in the contours of the motives and phrase, following their trajectory as we perceive the manner in which they are organized and articulated.

Let's look, for example, at crescendos and decrescendos, those places in a musical composition where things become gradually louder or softer. What defines a crescendo or its opposite is not merely an increase or decrease in volume. On the contrary, what informs these particular compositional elements is a certain *resistance* to the occurrence of getting louder or softer; we discern their effect, as it were, by putting up resistance to the accumulation or decrease of volume en route to a climax. An effective crescendo or decrescendo relies for its power on the gradual distension and adjudication of its volume. Thus it is not simply a question of getting louder or softer, but of cultivating a feeling for those opposing dynamic forces that would stand in the way of reaching the high point of any phrase, that is, its goal.

This, by the way, is how a fine actor conveys heartbreak with persuasive poignancy: not by bawling uncontrollably onstage, but precisely by making every effort *not* to, that is by attempting to stay in control and maintain dignity in the face of impossible emotional odds. In music, the same approach creates intonational and thus psychological tension, for in this context we experience the crescendo/decrescendo as a kind of overcoming that at once celebrates the gradual accumulation and ultimate release of that tension.

In Beethoven's day, the notion of overcoming adversity and victory in the face of struggle emerged as a central tenet of musical aesthetics.

Music, to a large extent, had become politicized, not only as a vehicle that was open to subjective reaction, and thus to any number of possible, if exogenous interpretations, but also through subtle changes in compositional process itself. Left to its own devices, rhythm, harmony, and form, while still abstractions, become ripe with meaning. Are the first, closely aligned four notes of Beethoven's Fifth Symphony, for example, really a symbol of "fate knocking at the door" as popular myth would have us believe? Perhaps. But in the larger context of the entire symphony, which recycles this motive ad infinitum, it may be that they speak with succinct expression to the notion of determination and overcoming. While these are matters perhaps best left to musical semiologists, they are nevertheless worthy of contemplation, as they have significant bearing on the way in which we experience and relate to music.

The grammar of engaged listening

It would be an oversimplification to say that *intonatsiia* refers simply to the differences between large and small intervals. Rather, it concerns the manner in which they, or any motivic configuration, are inflected and characterized. For example, *intonatsiia* can also refer to other modes of articulation, such as the way a musician enhances the opening pitch at the beginning of a phrase, perhaps by slightly lengthening it, like a skater pushing off onto the ice or a dancer inaugurating a *jeté*. This becomes, for our now shrewdly engaged ears, an *impulse*. It refers, too, to elements of surprise, suspense, and even violence (unexpected dissonances or syncopations, such as those that so frequently invigorate Beethoven or Shostakovich, for example); to the function of pedal points (the reiteration of a single note) to illustrate either stability or uncertainty; and not least, to the manner in which we perceive symbolic meaning. In short, intonatsiia embraces an array of expressive meaning that inform a work.

Intonatsiia encourages musicians to explore and exploit the expressive potential of every intervallic movement, to elaborate a musical grammar within the trajectory of a phrase, and to delineate and inflect carefully the character and shape of a motive. As listeners, we are equally capable of identifying and imaginatively engaging a work's many complexes of articulation as the music unfolds in time. It is the kind of listening that ought be cultivated with the greatest care, patience, and I dare say enchantment.

What intonatsiia produces is a mode of listening that migrates into every aspect of our listening habits and into a musician's playing. Here, expressive intent rules. Absolutely nothing, not even a scale, ought ever be taken for granted or dispatched mechanically, but should instead project a melodic attitude.

So far we've established that in its most fundamental sense, intonatsiia is all about what goes on in between the notes. It's something akin, you might say, to "reading between the lines" of a poem or a novel. It's the realm of affective inflection that conveys tension, longing, direction, and, on a subtler plane, the tendency of one pitch to gravitate toward another. On a larger scale, too, we've discerned that these same attributes likewise govern, though do not define in any specific material (that is, harmonic or rhythmic) category, the relationship between phrases, or even whole movements.

But is intonatsiia, when employed as a way of listening to music, in any way influenced by the instrument or the musical genre? Does it matter if a prelude of Bach is played on the harpsichord or on piano, or if Beethoven's Ninth Symphony is performed by a hundred players or by a far smaller ensemble?

Well, the simple answer is not so simple: yes and no. Thanks to the ability of every instrument except the piano, harpsichord, and percussion to sustain and intensify a single pitch en route to its neighbor, the average listener will at first find it easier to experience intonatsiia in orchestral and vocal music. After all, instrumental musicians provide much of the "synaptic" work already, filling in the gaps between the notes with discernible sound and volume. Whereas a pianist must convey pitch prolongation and intensification by imaginative means, since the moment any note is played on the piano the sound diminishes rapidly, a violinist, an oboist, or a singer takes command of the *material* elements of legato, for example—that is, the physical presence of sound in continuity; pitches literally hemorrhage one into the other.

Performers do more than recite or parrot a text. They engage it as they live in the moment; once onstage they abandon nothing of their curiosity or wonder. And as they are doing so, the informed listener is likewise engaged. Both performer and listener are constantly looking for something new in a journey of discovery that refuses to reify music, that is, to turn it into something frozen and inflexible. Those performers and listeners who refuse to be intimidated by musical experience are also those willing to embrace their vulnerability to its charms and to admit that there is always something new to discover. Music, thus allowed to present its own case, is now immune from the kind of routine, passive, and thoroughly disengaged listening that would disallow it to move into our psyches and the fiber of our being.

Of course, as a matter of preparation, a performer has laid out a musical work in detail, identifying its structural elements in an effort to strategize the interpretation. He has become cognizant of its harmonic goals, rhythmic trajectory, and the like. But by the time he goes on stage, he must be free *not* to anticipate what's about to happen next. This is the responsibility of a performer toward himself as well as his listeners: to clarify the compositional prosody and captivate everyone's ears in the interest of fulfilling musical experience. Just as an actor must "find" the words of the script as if he'd never read or heard them before, so must the musician do with the notes as he looks behind, between, and beyond them for meaning.

The French philosopher Roland Barthes described this process as "inscribing" oneself in the text, wherein reading is no less an active engagement than writing. Ideally, we should "write" what we read, reinventing the text as we "inscribe" ourselves dialectically within it. In so doing, we dissolve barriers that would otherwise separate the one activity from the other. And thus as listeners, too, we strive to participate in music in ways that are just as significant and intense as that of the performer himself.

To hear music is not enough; in order to gain the most from the experience, to satisfy our curiosity and whet our sensual appetites, we should heed Theodor W. Adorno's advice and listen *along with* the music. While there is no compelling need for listeners to identify any particular compositional event by its technical name (which would assume a level of training that most listeners do not have), we can however cultivate sensitivity to musical "events," that is, to those things in the musical text that jar, move, or strike us as strange. To paraphrase Barthes, we inscribe ourselves individually in the music.

Intonatsiia, then, may provide a key to understanding, listening, and performing music in the context of the conventions of the composer's era, and in accordance with his aesthetic philosophy as well as our own. Given the importance of intonatsiia to musical experience, I will continue to explore its potential throughout this survey of Beethoven's magnificent nine.

Context and Significance

With few exceptions, scholars and devotees alike have singled out Beethoven's Third ("Eroica") and Fifth symphonies as pivotal, not only to his development as a composer, but in the history of Western music. As we shall see, both symphonies, composed in what has been referred to alternately as his "heroic" period or phase (an artificial construct whose efficacy is dubious, given Beethoven himself used the word "heroic" on the title pages of only two compositions, the piano sonata Op. 26 and the "Eroica" Symphony), aspired to a kind of musical apotheosis. They also gave legitimacy to a new aesthetic concept, idealism, which celebrated contemplation of art as it paid respects to abstraction. Commensurate with Beethoven's emergence, a new social and aesthetic landscape took root, and within the first years of the nineteenth century, musical perception changed forever. Music assumed an importance and purpose that, until then, it did not enjoy among thinkers or the public. It became an occasion for reflection as well as a symbol of community.

While it would be difficult, and probably ill-advised, to dispute this widely held opinion about the Third and Fifth symphonies, it would be equally unwise to diminish the significance of the First Symphony, composed a few years earlier in 1800. Its importance cannot be underestimated. But as the Age of Enlightenment drew to its close at the dawn of the nineteenth century, this work gave voice to a wholly new aesthetic that contradicted the artistic imprimatur of the previous century.

For the first time in the history of Western music, symphonic music, which Beethoven liberated in many ways, took precedence over opera.

By 1800, artists and thinkers had at last conceded that music, absent the specificity of an accompanying text, had something to convey on its own terms. They had accepted the idea that music was a language in its own right, albeit an abstract one (an idea that would be challenged again more than a hundred years later by a new discipline, musical semiotics), and that its implicit ambiguity was precisely its strength.

Where words set to music could convey something specific, wordless music could be interpreted in any number of ways. In the eighteenth century, this ambiguity was viewed as a disadvantage that only poetry or a libretto could overcome. As revelers welcomed the new century in January 1800, the embrace of ambiguity was already under way. At long last, the symphony—as an independent genre no less artistically expressive than opera—had arrived. It was just as this newly embraced idea gained favor that Beethoven's First Symphony in C Major made such a profound impression in Vienna.

It is perhaps no accident that Beethoven was thirty years old— young by today's standards but somewhere beyond middle age in his day—when he composed it in 1800 (though he left sketches of it going back as early as 1795). His resolve to wait as long as he did may not have been due entirely to either aesthetic considerations or any lack of confidence in his own abilities, but to economics. The publication of an orchestral score in its entirety was rare in the eighteenth century and the chances of its distribution for widespread performance were exceptionally slim. Indeed, until the 1820s, the publishing industry's customary and usual practice in this genre was to print and distribute only the individual parts.

The concerns that informed the music-publishing industry's agenda were hardly murky but likewise economic. Before 1800, the public and men of letters alike viewed purely instrumental works as too abstract, and also as inferior to opera and vocal music. Opera, with its emphasis on word and story—like cinema in the twentieth century—was all the rage, while performances of symphonies were confined to either special public presentations arranged and paid for by the composer, or offered as spirited entertainments commissioned by the aristocracy for their private pleasure.

Thus publishers were unwilling to risk money on anything as essentially unpopular, in comparison to vocal music, as a symphony. They knew well there was no substantial market for it and that the publication of works only rarely heard would fail to return their investment as handsomely as a popular opera. What's more, throughout the 1700s, public concerts devoted to new orchestral works were often offered free of charge and financed by the composer himself. No doubt this was the most effective way for both aspiring and established composers to cultivate the public's favor and attract the attention of new patrons. While Beethoven was never a man to sacrifice artistic ideals for commercial considerations, he could not have been unaware of these circumstances, and in any case, his early publishers treated him no differently than any other artist.

While today it may seem odd to imagine a symphonic work performed in someone's home, the orchestra of Beethoven's early years was nothing like the densely populated ensembles we know today. Smaller ensembles of thirty or forty musicians were sufficient. Orchestras were rarely provided an opportunity to rehearse, in any case, and composers, who usually conducted their own music, were compelled to make the best of a precarious situation.

As wealthy aristocrats filled their glittering palatial ballrooms with two hundred or more bejeweled guests to hear what was then new music, composers (Beethoven among them) relied upon the patronage of the wealthy. But amid the silk cuffs and powdered wigs, ornate embroidery, and silver candelabras, something new was in the air. While words had specific meaning and could convey an idea to anyone with precision, the emotional ambiguity of instrumental music began to capture popular imagination. And so, while well-heeled guests ate off gold plate in rococo dining rooms, and fussy, bemonocled fops complimented each other on the quality of their newest Indian silks, music began to aspire, for them as well as the bourgeoisie, to the "level" of poetry.

For more than a century, the autonomy of musical form was dismissed as secondary in importance to music that was accompanied by a text, such as opera. Words with music fulfilled the expectations of a society that cherished language as the sole proprietor of musical meaning. Instrumental compositions, on the other hand, were largely pleasing entertainments and little more. The overall sentiment was that anything as pure as instrumental music couldn't possibly communicate the beauty brought to life by a good story set to music. Composers were expected to yield to the widely accepted notion that music's most important function was to assimilate the rhythms and inflections of speech and to mimic the sounds of nature.

This so-called mimesis assumed extraordinary importance in the music of the eighteenth century. But as the Age of Enlightenment, inspired by the achievements of the French Revolution, came to a close at the end of that century, music itself had evolved into something more compelling; having attained to autonomy, music no longer depended on singers, theater, or words to make its point. The parroting of nature and grammar diminished in importance. Music had had found its own voice, and also something of its political potential.

While only a few decades earlier, Mozart's wholly original symphonies were rarely performed and Haydn's were known largely to his colleagues and patrons (though bits and pieces of the former's operas and the latter's choral music were hummed by the man in the street), Beethoven's music exploited the ambiguity of wordless music. With the emergence of Idealism, the intelligentsia—and the public, too—gave music its due. In its wordlessness, music could be interpreted as being capable of embracing a much wider gamut of human experience and emotions, from dread and terror to exaltation and wonder. The idea that music could be something more substantial and worthy of contemplation, as opposed to merely pleasing, was significant.

In the baroque and early classical eras, philosophers and composers alike embraced the relationship of language and music as being the most valuable principle of musical aesthetics. Not only the spoken word but also the rhythms of speech and the grammatical structures of language became singular objectives that composers attempted to render by analogy. In this context, phrases mimicked linguistic structures, while dynamics mimicked the sounds of nature. A tremolo was just as readily interpreted as thunder as pizzicato was rain, and even punctuation was codified in sound. While it may be a generalization that a sforzando, for example, could prevail as a kind of exclamation point and a rest could become a pregnant pause, devices of this sort informed compositional vocabulary.

In the century preceding Beethoven, the overwhelming majority of composers competed with each other to see who could most effectively manipulate that vocabulary. Court composers were, after all, paid to please their masters, and those who felt comfortable doing just that made a decent living. Where the rare genius of Mozart and Haydn set the stage for future musical innovation, most composers were ruled by an aesthetic disposition that fetishized the relationship of speech to music. From the perspective of eighteenth-century ears, nothing could compete with the human voice, which could spin out an attractive tune at the same time it used poetry and prose to tell a stirring tale.

Beethoven's first symphony, then, was every bit as important to musical culture as his later works in the same genre, and not only for strictly musical reasons. Though it would be easy to attribute the publication of the full score to Beethoven's increasing popularity, the decision by one group of British publishers to do so in a limited edition in 1803 brings up a larger issue. This was an admission by the status quo that the public taste and tolerance for new music had changed for good.

Mind you, the coincidence was not due to cause and effect; it was not only Beethoven's music that persuaded the publishing industry to rethink its policies, but the intellectual climate in Napoleonic Europe. Post-Enlightenment idealism gave way to a new way of thinking about and listening to music abstractly, which is to say, apart from any explicit accompanying story sung or spoken. What came to be viewed as crucial to musical truth was its content: form, harmony, rhythm, and counter-point. A new appreciation for musical complexity began to inform the way people related to music. Music composed for and played by a single instrument or ensemble was now considered worthy of serious atten-tion, and not as an occasion for passive entertainment. It had become the sonorous, wordless embodiment of community and idea, and thus an experience worthy of embrace.

Yet it was precisely what was elusive about "truth" that caused the public to reinvent its relationship to music. In the absence of words, music of this kind—lengthy, complex, and overwhelming—demanded

more of the average listener. The emphasis was no longer on its entertainment value and spontaneous effect, that is, its strictly subjective
emotional impact, as it had been in the previous century, but on its
autonomy and substance. In order to fathom music from within, to
determine its strategies, to grasp its contradictions and elusive goals,
and to interpret its symbolic, psychological, and political "meaning,"
the listener was now obliged to pay closer attention. It was no longer
enough to listen to music passively; it required a kind of participatory
listening that was fully engaged. In the mid-twentieth century, Theodor
W. Adorno described this as "listening along" with the music; that is, a
way of following compositional events intelligibly as they unfold.

Yet even with this leap toward an enhanced and intelligible manner
of listening, contradictions abounded. Perhaps this was an unforeseen
consequence of another newly accepted element of musical aesthetics, to
wit, synthesis, wherein contradictory ideas could be developed in play
with each other. While E. T. A. Hoffman, in his metaphor-rich critique
of Beethoven's Fifth, dismissed the average music lover as incapable of
disciplined listening, members of the public could have cared less; they
were enamored of music that moved them in a way that nothing had
before. This clash between intellectual and popular culture set the stage
for a new kind of music criticism—what I call musical journalism—that
marginalized erudition and critique of music itself in favor of extolling
its performance for an adoring public.

Thus in spite of the new appreciation of instrumental music, which
in an ideal world free of commercial interests might have gone on
to inform the way the public views classical music today, this new
emphasis on external considerations ironically served to revive the
idea of music as entertainment. Contemplation and analysis were left
to the experts, while the power of music to please or sadden through
mnemic association never entirely vanished, as the intelligentsia of the
day had hoped.

Symphony No. 1 in C Major, Op. 21

2 Flutes, 2 Oboes, 2 Clarinets (C), 2 Bassoons, 2 Horns (C, F), 2 Trumpets (C), Timpani, Violins, Violas, Cellos, Basses

Date of composition circa 1799; exact period of composition unknown

First performance in Vienna, April 2, 1800

Dedicated to Baron Gottfried van Swieten

First movement: Adagio molto; Allegro con brio
Second movement: Andante cantabile con moto
Third movement: Menuetto: Allegro molto e vivace
Fourth movement: Finale: Adagio; Allegro molto e vivace

What a remarkable effect Beethoven's First Symphony must have had at its initial performance in Vienna on April 2, 1800. For one thing, it marked the young composer's debut as a symphonist. Until then it was largely his piano music that delighted the aristocracy as much as it did the common man and raised the collective eyebrows of the cognoscenti.

Though very much in keeping with the formal norms of classical composition, the First Symphony's real abundance lies in the sheer audacity of its ideas. There is a motoric vivacity about it that sets it apart from anything that preceded it. Its melodies and motivic organization, while conforming to the relatively short periodic phrases favored at the time, were not only a model of economy, but something more: they were bold, they were adroitly characterized, and they articulated, with unabashed fervor, the sensibility of its composer.

If I may digress for a moment, I would like to propose changing the paradigm for the discussion and analysis of music. For those who may not be so comfortable with technical terminology, no matter how fundamental or arcane, have no fear. While I could certainly refer to the home key of any tonal composition as that of the tonic, or to its closest relations as the dominant, subdominant, and mediant (the common terminology of harmonic analysis), I prefer, for the purposes of this book, to raise another kind of question: How is it possible for our ears recognize a musical event as it happens in real time, and once we do, how do we determine its significance? Are some events more significant than others? And while it's all well and good to identify the various elements of a musical composition by name, what use will that kind of exercise be to listeners who are unable to do so?

So as to appreciate and recognize significant compositional events as they occur within the musical fabric, it may prove more productive to focus our attention on both the rhythmic and melodic progression of the work at hand. In other words, what we ought to ask ourselves as listeners is not to which key this or that chord belongs, or how the imposition of a Schenker graph would illuminate both form and harmonic structure, but something even more essential. And that is: Where are things—by which I mean the melodies and rhythms—going; where did they come from in the first place; and how did they get there? By what visceral or aural means can listeners untrained in the vocabulary and complexes of music find their way home and back?

Think of it this way: all of us know very well our own homes. We know how they are laid out, where the furniture is, where we've made open space or indifferently created clutter. If we are particularly well organized, we may even know what lurks in the darkest recesses of every closet and behind the rakes and shovels in the garage. Even during a power failure, when everything is thrown into total darkness, we can find our way around, though the nearsighted among us might benefit from a candle or two. We may be able to find our way about easily enough in such circumstances, though the gentle illumination of a small candle, even in a familiar place, would be welcome and would prevent us from stumbling over the unforeseen.

While this may sound like the stuff of an Alfred Hitchcock thriller, there is a certain analogy to a mystery novel that comes into play. Just as Agatha Christie keeps us on our toes in anticipation of whodunit, providing clues elaborated by the heroes and villains who populate her texts, so does Beethoven proffer information, in musical categories. These musical clues are *motives*, the musical equivalent to literary characters.

We can easily recognize a motive, no matter how brief, by its rhythm, pitch organization, melody, or mood. Beethoven is such a skillful composer that he never fails to harvest details that allow us to follow his train of thought. While he has organized, with exquisite finesse, the parts of his compositions into an intelligible whole, he eventually leads us back to where we began, though on the way there he has developed, varied, and elaborated his materials. Eventually the home key—which, as we shall see, is the compositional equivalent of the sun—having traversed its compositional sky, reappears on this sonorous horizon and reminds us again that we've made it home.

For our part, as intonatsiia-savvy listeners, we strive to cultivate our listening habits, inscribing ourselves within the musical activity. Complexity in art music, that is, the myriad parts, rhythms, harmonies, and not least, relationships of each of these to the other, is hardly something to be feared, but to be embraced. That one listener, untrained in the context of analysis, finds himself unable to name this or that particle is unimportant, because in the end, it's really a matter of listening with open ears and an open heart.

To this end we can, each and every one of us, decipher musical form, whether in its smallest incarnation (the motive), which is nothing more than a fragment of a larger picture, or in its largest array, be it a fugue or a sonata. Repetition is vital to understanding the architecture of musical form. Thus it is not without purpose, both structural and pragmatic, that the laws of composition have traditionally demanded, de rigueur, the repetition of whole sections. As we listen to music, doing our best to follow its myriad melodies, fascinating rhythms, and changing harmonies, patterns emerge. These patterns embed themselves in our perception and memory. It is to these patterns that our ears become accustomed. With this, and the composer's help, the destiny of each motive evolves before our eyes (or should I say, our ears). Finally it takes its place within the larger formal context it informs, influences, and ultimately helps to create.

First movement: Adagio molto; Allegro con brio

The opening of this symphony makes no apologies in exploiting a certain tonal ambiguity, if only by suggestion. However, it is not nearly as ambiguous as it first appears. The opening Adagio, which inaugurates the work in F major en route to G major, both relative keys, gives way to a poignant soliloquy of sorts, although one that belies even that description given its multivalence of voices. It is not only the key that creates a sense of anticipation, in the first four measures, but the drawn-out chords, presided over by flutes and oboes drifting from strong to weak—from *forte* to *piano*—just as the composer indicates. In this opening hush, Beethoven engenders a musical climate that breathes uncertainty as to where it might be going.

Only four measures into this lovely introduction he introduces an ardent, stepwise melody in the violins that gently articulates a mood at once consoling and conciliatory, as if to dismiss its tenuous uncertainty and to assure us that, in the end, everything is going to be all right. It is an unusually personal, though generous, disclosure that betrays its composer's most heartfelt sentiments without a hint of strident sentimentality.

This entire introduction spans only twelve bars before the strings introduce a somber, ascending G major scale, which plummets suddenly in a flurry of four descending thirty-second-notes. Landing squarely in the next bar and in unison on a single pitch, C, the first movement settles here into its home key.

But here I have broken my promise not to use technical terminology. So let's turn back the clock for a moment and see how we got to this new event, that is, to the establishment of the "home key." What does that really mean?

If you think of a work of tonal music—music that depends for its very existence on the organization of its parts into tonal regions, or keys, and their relationships—as a kind of solar system, with planets, asteroids, meteors, light, and infinite space, you will also have to conclude that somewhere or other there lurks a sun, too. And just about everything in this musically construed solar system orbits around that sun.

What I am getting at here is that the home key is akin to the sun, and its purpose is similar. The home (tonic) key is a kind of sonorous landscape that gives sanctuary to the all the parts of a composition and welcomes them home when they drift away or go off on their own into other keys. This tonal center exerts its own kind of gravitational pull, too. Everything in its sphere of influence moves inexorably toward it, and we experience this movement as fulfilling. The moment we return to the home key we sense a certain satisfaction, as if things were meant to return there all along. In turn, the parts of the composition—its rhythmically organized notes and motives—are irradiated by the heat of this musical sun, which not only envelops its progeny in its ever-present rays, but assures them of its power and permanence.

At the conclusion of the endearing introduction, the melodious strains of the languid Adagio melt away in an ascending scale only to pounce with vigor on to the Allegro molto. As it reaches its highest note, a G, its intonation realizes itself and conveys itself, to any attentive listener, as both definitive and conclusive. On this prolonged pitch, our musical sun begins to rise and only moments later peers over the horizon, though in this case the horizon is an entirely new, contrasting section, Allegro molto.

This is an event of significance. After the slow, stately, and tender lyricism of the introduction, Beethoven suspends things for a bit on G (the dominant), a related key held in esteem by C major. He then pulls us into the domain of the C major, as if to say "All is well; we have arrived," and pounces on its principal pitch, C. The feeling that we have done so—and no one needs an advanced degree to recognize a sudden change in mood and texture—is not entirely subjective. On the contrary, it is an objective fact, just at that point where the uncertain sentiments of the Adagio evolve into the bold, confident motivic statement that opens the Allegro molto, that Beethoven leads us home, as it were. And "home" is the central key of the piece. It constitutes an event, musically speaking, because, after much prolongation and evasion in related tonalities, C major at last and definitively reveals itself, and it does so within the context of a bright and energetic new tempo.

With the introduction of this vivacious new material in the home key, Beethoven has the orchestra stay put for a few beats on that single tonic pitch, C. Then, with unabashed assurance, it gives way to an energetic three-note motive beginning on G and ascending to C. This motive announces itself as an independent cell characterized in a distinct dotted rhythm (long–short–long).

Beethoven was one composer who took nothing for granted; for him, every note, every phrase, every motive had meaning. Even a cursory examination of his notebooks and manuscripts discloses an artist who was never satisfied with what he had just written, the proof of which are the innumerable scrawls, annotations, and corrections that so frequently pepper his scores. Even here, this miniature motive becomes something more; it becomes the "motor" that drives the entire movement forward. Within the space of a few measures, Beethoven wastes no time intensifying it in a six-bar phrase that hammers out that single tonic pitch (C) again and again. Keep in mind that throughout this movement, and indeed, the entire symphony, Beethoven runs a particularly tight ship: the relationship of that one pitch, C, to the other two notes in the motivic figure, namely G and B-natural, form a clue to the work's mysteries. It is as if everything orbits around that one note.

Any numbers of theoretical treatises, most notably those of twentieth-century German theorist Heinrich Schenker, set forth, in essence, that most compositions revolve around one single pitch or a group of pitches. That is admittedly a gross oversimplification of Schenker's complex theories, but in this case, it will do. You might say that, in Beethoven's First, for example, all roads lead not only back to the home key, but to a single pitch, C. Even in those many places where the music migrates into relative or foreign keys, the essential motivic patterns, perspective, and intervallic proportions remain the same. This understanding is useful because it provides us, in the absence of a score or any specific musical training, a kind of aural road map.

A charming second theme, characterized in a descending diatonic scale of five notes, emerges as dialogue between the oboes and flutes. A few bars later, as the clarinets and bassoons lend their support from below, the violins, picking up the theme, enter the musical conversation. It's a playful affair, unsullied by anxiety or the dramatic outbursts that Beethoven would so masterfully introduce in his later music.

But wait! Just as the *exposition* (the first part of a form in which the presentation of all the major themes is set forth) is about to draw to a close, Beethoven ushers in the cellos with the same theme, but this time the message is more serious, as if to introduce a certain gravitas into the musical texture. A lone oboe sings out plaintively above, in anticipation of the re-introduction of the original three-note motive that inaugurated this Allegro con brio.

As these themes roll over into the development section, which expands and varies the material, Beethoven combines the first and second themes as a means to intensify their meaning. But now the flutes, oboes, and bassoon take over the original dotted motive, like relaying racers in a sportive match, handing this abbreviated yet important theme one to the other in a spirited interplay. But Beethoven doesn't allow this woodwind team too much freedom. Just below, the violins have fastened themselves into rather relentless groupings of repeated staccato notes, which not only drive things forward, but also, in their forceful-ness, restrain the playful interchange in the woodwinds above.

The recapitulation—the section that recycles with slight differences the motivic ideas presented in the exposition—ensues. This first move-ment in Beethoven's First Symphony comes to its exciting, optimistic conclusion in a resounding affront of C major chords, laid out over twelve entire bars as descending arpeggios and finally, in the conclud-ing six measures, as sonorous chords. But the last chord is *not* the end of the piece. Beethoven indicates nearly two whole bars of rests—that is, of silence. Once again this can hardly be interpreted as empty space or meaningless silence, but as music without notes; it is the transition to the next movement, and, as such, the rests create a kind of frame, distinguishing what has just passed from what is to follow. (This is all the more reason that audiences should avoid breaking into applause at the end of a movement, or immediately upon the conclusion of an entire piece; more often than not more remains, and the work is not yet over!)

But the word *recapitulation* and indeed, the concept behind it, some-how fails to capture the idea of form in its most vibrant incarnation. If there is one reason that all the fuss over form alienates the nonexpert listener, it's because form is not and never has been something dead, laid out flat as if it were merely lines and figures on a piece of paper. As Theodor W. Adorno put it, form "catches fire on content," and that it does. From this perspective, then, form is less a matter of architectural dissemination (though in musical terms, the division of so many notes and rhythms into cohesively designed sections is easy enough to discern, even by untrained ears) than it is a fluid, ongoing, dynamic process wherein ideas are developed, elaborated, and propelled forward inevitably toward some specific goal.

Let's step back for a moment, as this movement makes us aware of something particularly important: the essence of Beethoven's musical language. Even here, in his first excursion into symphonic form, Beethoven demonstrates more than a simple liking for the role of sforzandos, which punctuate the orchestral texture like so many shakes of the fist. Indeed, the imposition of such sudden but frequent dynamic contrasts is more often than not informed by syncopated motives and rhythms. It is no accident that, in such places, Beethoven assigns his sforzandos to the second beat in any given measure, that is, to a weak beat. This contradicts the natural tendency of the first and third beats in 4/4 time to absorb a certain emphasis, or weight.

To say that this compulsion or even fetish on Beethoven's part is symbolic of upsetting the status quo invites speculation, but its function in compositional categories is entirely autonomous. While we can analyze the number of such incidents and determine their overall structural role within the musical tapestry, what matters in the end is something else: how it affects us, moves in on us, and alters our perception of time passing. After all, the time signature of 4/4, where there are exactly four beats to every bar, can become, for lesser composers who extol rhythmic regularity as a virtue, little more than a receptacle for notes piled on one after the other.

For Beethoven, that would be unimaginable. A composer of sophomoric marches he was not! In any case, as we listen, it's useful to understand how these sforzandos affect our perceptions; what they imply occurs between the notes. Here is yet another occasion in which intonatsiia, as a tool for acute listening, comes in handy. Within the relatively thin orchestration of this strings-and-woodwinds-saturated movement, these now vigorous, now unsettling dynamic elements take on heightened value. We hear in them something of Beethoven's impatience with things as they normally are or should be and his determination to shake things up and grab our attention.

In Beethoven, "sforzando" is a distinct accentuation that can and often does occur in any dynamic context, be it a *forte* or a *piano*. But in every case where the sforzando occurs, there is or ought not be any rhapsodic diminishment of its affect; there can be no diminuendo, willfully and rhapsodically imposed, en route from the accented note to the unaccented one. It's simply *forte* and then, immediately following, *piano*.

What we as listeners perceive in this case is a genuine musical event, no matter how brief, that is akin to the silence after a storm. A Beethoven sforzando thrills as much as it unnerves us, and in combination with the syncopated rhythms, which so often host them in his music, we are thrown off base, as it were, and into a realm of anxiety and expectation.

Second movement: Andante cantabile con moto

This lovely and inspired movement is nothing if not an extended song of sorts that blossoms into something heftier, though hardly any less gracious. The first melody is a motivic fragment, which Beethoven skillfully weaves into something mobile and vivacious, and eventually envelops in a fugal web.

The principal theme is derivative, echoing both the first and second principal themes of the previous Allegro. Like that one, it also establishes itself with an interval of a major fourth, from C to F (the dotted motive in the first movement traversed G to C in a dotted motive), and then a lilting dotted figure that descends in a scale from B-flat to E-natural.

The violins carry the tune throughout, though the flutes pay homage to it in unison toward the end of the exposition, where kettledrums, murmuring in *pianissimo*, accompany a gracious convoy of triplets. But there is nothing in the least belligerent about the percussion here, or the manner in which Beethoven puts it to work. Its role is merely supportive.

Beethoven chose the key of F major for this Andante, the subdominant of C major. Is this key choice important? Well, yes and no. So let's digress a bit and take a brief look at the meaning of key relationships, though without embroiling ourselves in the complexities these can sometimes survey. For those to whom the very idea of a key is as foreign as the Cyrillic alphabet might be to non-Russians, don't fret.

For centuries there has been a widely held idea that every key, like the indigenous culture of a country, has a wholly autonomous character and disposition. Given that every key, major and minor, is based on identical internal relationships (that is, the manner in which the notes are arranged in relation to each other, separated by whole and half tones), this idea seems a purely subjective abstraction. Nevertheless, since the baroque era, certain keys have convinced listeners and professional musicians alike that they possess immanent properties. F major and B-flat major, for example, are thought to evoke, by as yet some as yet unexplained principle, a placid, bucolic atmosphere ideally suited for the evocation of nature effects. F-sharp major and A major are viewed as exceptionally bright or sunny keys wholly disposed toward music that is at once brilliant and martial, while D-sharp minor, as more than one Russian romantic composer would discern, held forth as something moody and oceanic.

Whatever case can be made for or against it, the idea of subjective association was certainly not lost on Beethoven. Here, in this dignified Andante, an easygoing processional of sorts gently exfoliates within the context of the sparse orchestration, creating a musical atmosphere that is at once dulcet and unruffled. This begs the question: Could Beethoven just as easily have accomplished this in another key, something far removed from C major, such as F-sharp major? Certainly he could have, but the effect, in relation to the entire movement that preceded it, and that which follows, would have been noticeable. Something of the aforementioned "betweenness," not only that which governs the space separating individual notes, but whole movements, would have affected our sensibility in subtle ways.

Third movement: Menuetto: Allegro molto e vivace
(CD Track 1)

In this lively movement, Beethoven owes much to Haydn and Mozart, who cultivated the minuet's formal conventions. But in this work, he also parts ways with these earlier composers, disavowing the leisurely pace that had characterized the minuet for a century. Here, Beethoven foreshadows an innovation of his own, the scherzo, or more accurately, the imposition of a scherzo, instead of a minuet within a symphony.

For more than a century before Beethoven was born in 1770, the minuet was a popular dance, and it was given to a rather leisurely tempo. It gained widespread acceptance and even adulation at the court of Louis XIV, who is said to have been an agile dancer himself. The minuet was a binary form characterized by triple meter—that is, three beats to the bar—and the overall regularity of its rhythmic organization, wherein its melodies and motivic materials were rendered consistent in four-bar phrases. There was nothing particularly shocking about the minuet, as it could be relied upon as an apt and elegant accompaniment for dancing in rococo ballrooms.

But the minuet, for Beethoven, became opportunity. Infusing this once pleasant but ever-so-bourgeois dance form with abundant energy, Beethoven transformed it into something new, a heightened confection that was both brusque and humorous. It became the scherzo. In this, his First Symphony, he pays homage to tradition by continuing to call it a minuet, but it really is not; it is already a scherzo.

Mozart and Haydn had already expanded the minuet to include a contrasting section, or trio. But Beethoven takes things just a step further, heightening the tempo and urgency of the form so forcibly that no human could possibly dance to it. Rapid modulations dovetail with each other in the context of the work's overall upward trajectory.

From the opening salvo, this movement makes its mark as a genuine scherzo; it is nothing if not audacious. Opening with a simple but vigorously framed ascending G major scale distended over eight bars, the violins, as custodians of this marvelous theme, take flight, landing promptly, in unison with the strings and flutes, on a resounding G before repeating it all. But then, suddenly, Beethoven introduces something a just bit ominous, by lowering the sixth degree of the scale. Without warning, and fewer than ten bars into the work (0:10 in the accompanying recording), A-natural turns into A-flat, giving this energetic concoction a brief taste of a minor mode.

On the way back to the original theme, this time spread out with even greater confidence by the violins, violas, and woodwinds that share the theme in unison, Beethoven exploits the affective uncertainty of the transitional material. This he does simply but effectively, thus creating tension and allowing a sequence of repeated notes to prevail in the strings, which rise, with a certain tenaciousness, in half steps (0:24). The timpani, too, share in the musical action, lending their support, like foot soldiers, to a charming theme now made courageous in character.

As if to throw off our sensibilities even more, Beethoven fawns over the last bars of the section, enveloping them at first in pugnacious sforzandos on the downbeats (0:39) and then in a sequence of syncopations, wherein the emphasis then shifts stealthlike to the third beat in each bar (0:43). This sort of dramatic emphasis, wherein syncopated rhythms affixed to hemiolas come into play, had already become one of Beethoven's imaginative trademarks in his piano sonatas and string quartets.

Given the importance of syncopation in Beethoven's musical language, let's have a closer look. But don't panic; no one need flee at the mention of hemiola! Though the word itself may sound as if it refers to a blood disease, it is a relatively simple compositional device. Strictly speaking, a hemiola is a substitute. Just as a single substitute teacher may be occasionally called in to your kid's gym class to take over for two instructors—say, a coach and a trainer—a hemiola fits in two measures (or notes) of equal value to replace three measures (or notes) of equal value, or vice versa. In the case of this minuet, Beethoven ties quarter-notes across the bar (0:43 in the recording) and, in so doing, turns two evidently separate notes into a single one. The emphasis falls squarely on the first of the tied notes, which is coincidentally the weak beat of each bar. The effect is jarring, as it disrupts both our expectations and conditioned response to the rhythmic certainty of a conventional downbeat. The net effect is that of something impetuous, even strident, which at once throws the music forward as it intensifies its affect.

Given the brevity of the movement and its run-along pace, the sheer number of modulations is astonishing. Many have described it as emblematic of the composer's humor and his willingness to snub his nose at the establishment. That may be, but it may say as much about Beethoven's impatience toward, if not intolerance of, a form that represented the very things he sought to challenge and eventually change. The minuet, at least in its first French incarnation, represented not only the glib pretensions of the aristocracy, but also bourgeois self-satisfaction; it was nothing if not an emblem of things the way they always were and as the ruling classes hoped they would forever remain.

As time went on, though, the minuet absorbed something of the idiosyncratic rhythmic and melodic identities of related dances. For one thing, as its popularity increased and moved beyond French borders into central Europe in the early eighteenth century, its lively tempo slowed to accommodate the influence of rural contra dances, quadrilles, and, in Austria, the yodel. Once danced and domesticated by the corpulent Louis XIV (whose obesity is said to have been responsible for its slowing down!), the minuet was eventually co-opted by commoners. This intermingling of refined form with the popular conventions of music and dance transformed it from a model of polite engagement to an occasion for ribald revelry.

Into that milieu steps Beethoven, wily, rude, imaginative, disciplined, and uncompromising, turning the poor old minuet on its head. He overtook the form with such uncommon mastery as to be able to present it, jujitsu-like, as a kind of personal affront to the establishment, yet without compromising either compositional procedure or the structural demands that the minuet itself demanded. Thus, with the transformation of minuet into a vivacious dance-rocket, which he had yet to label *scherzo*, his mission was complete. Hector Berlioz extolled this movement as "the only real novelty" in the entire symphony. "Novelty" is an understatement; perhaps "genius" is more apt.

The ensuing trio (1:35) is a fanciful affair ushered in with a placid hush of woodwinds and horns. Interrupted almost immediately by a wistful breeze of ascending scales in the violins and violas, they come together in a jovial dialogue that might be viewed as contradicting the movement's initial rambunctiousness. The gentle chiding continues for only a minute or so until it is repeated, and we are given over once again to the A section (2:53). Whatever subtle changes occur in the ensuing da capo, that is, the repetition of the first section, are largely up to the imagination of the conductor, who, if he is like Furtwängler, is allergic to rote playing.

Before we move on, a word about interpretation: Beethoven modifies the opening notes of the movement with dots placed squarely over each one of them. What does this mean? Well, at first glance, a dot placed over (not beside!) a note is an indication to play it staccato. There has long been a widespread misconception, among untrained ears and even among certain professional musicians, of the meaning of these kinds of dots and indeed the concept of staccato itself. There are those who naively continue to believe that the very meaning of staccato is to eviscerate a note of all its implicit breadth and resonance. This ersatz conception wherein staccato is interpreted to mean, quite wrongly, that the note it modifies ought be radically shortened and played as if it were pinched is unfortunate. Staccato is not staccatissimo, a device only rarely used and almost never in the baroque and classical canon.

On the contrary, staccato was assigned its meaning in the baroque era, which understood it to mean nothing more or less than the cancellation of its opposite, to wit, legato. Given that instrumental music took its cue and inspiration from vocal music and did its best to reproduce the properties of the human voice, it was in fact a smooth and connected style of playing, or legato, that prevailed. The imposition of staccato dots was only an instruction to separate the notes; the point was to distinguish each pitch from its neighbors on either side. Thus, a note with a dot over it can and should be allowed to breathe, to expand, and to vibrate, but with the understanding that it must also be distinctly separated from that which precedes it and that which follows it. Or as one particularly ribald piano teacher of mine once amusingly put it, "Lift and separate!"

Pay careful attention, then, to the way in which Wilhelm Furtwängler so adroitly and reasonably approaches this passage as he brings the theme into focus. He is a musician who is enormously respectful of the letter as well as the spirit of the score. As he ever so gently and almost imperceptibly accents the downbeats on the half-notes, he meticulously separates the notes one from the other. But as you will observe, he also allows them their full value. There is no pinching or scratching of bow against string, but a subtle lengthening of the staccato notes in the most vocal manner. A singer, after all, cannot perform with a closed throat that chokes on every pitch; no matter what the length of the note in play, air must pass through the vocal cords for sound to be produced. It ought to be no different, aesthetically speaking, for any other instrument, and it is the responsibility of the performer to make certain that such details are properly and persuasively conveyed.

Fourth movement: Adagio; Allegro molto e vivace

Once again, Beethoven challenges our expectations, and wastes no time doing so in the first seven bars of this jaunty rondo. The introductory Adagio presents a puzzle straightaway when the entire orchestra, with woodwinds, timpani, and brass now ablaze, blurts out a lone G in *fortissimo* unison. What does it all mean?

This presumptuous nod to the dominant tonality (on the fifth degree of the C major scale) is no accident: it sets the tone for the odd, even timorous attitude that infuses the few measures that follow. Again, just as he had in the minuet, Beethoven abstracts a portion of a rising C major scale that he moves forward only in increments. At its outset he proffers first a motivic fragment of three ascending notes, followed in rapid succession by groups of four, five, six, and finally seven notes. While brief rests separate each individual group, they never stop moving. On the contrary, they compel us to listen through the rests as they shift themselves ever so cautiously from the opening G to F, the subdominant fourth degree of the scale. When at last these consecutive figures alight on that single pitch, F, staying put there for a bit under a fermata, something of the confident assurance of the opening has already vanished. The mood is now one of uncertainty, but only for a moment. With the introduction of the principal theme of the Allegro molto, we have regained our footing.

The presentation of the principal theme, a model of classical decorum, is unfettered by overt modulations or any other harmonic surprises. While the woodwinds, supported by timpani, hold forth in thirds and sixths in reference to things bucolic, the strings are given over entirely to brusque scale passages, which intensify, both in volume and through their metrical organization. The second theme, too, bears a certain resemblance to that of the first movement, though here its mood, modified by two-note slurs over the *bar line*, is anxious, not placid.

As to be expected in what might have been a totally unremarkable movement in anyone else's hands, the development is a minefield of scale fragments, again given over wholly to the strings, which tumble gently, now ascending, now descending, one into the other in a cheerful dialogue and in friendly competition. The coda, mixing the scale fragments with the two principal themes, follows the recapitulation's double-dotted thrust toward a spirited cadence on the dominant. The final twelve bars, played *fortissimo* (though the final bar is entirely a rest!), bring the symphony to a proud and definitive conclusion.

Symphony No. 2
in D Major, Op. 36

2 Flutes, 2 Oboes, 2 Clarinets (A), 2 Bassoons,
2 Horns (D, E), 2 Trumpets (D), Timpani, Violins,
Violas, Cellos, Basses

Composed in 1802; first performance April 5,
1803, at the Theater-an-der-Wien, Vienna

Dedicated to Prince Karl Lichnowsky

First movement: Adagio molto; Allegro con brio
Second movement: Larghetto
Third movement: Scherzo: Allegro
Fourth movement: Allegro molto

In October 1802, a despondent Beethoven, having reconciled himself after six years to his deafness, wrote his celebrated Heiligenstadt Testament. This extraordinary document, though ostensibly his last will and the fruit of his depression, gave eloquent voice to his self-doubt. But it also set forth, in its defiant yet confessional tone, his refusal to abandon his musical gifts, which in his view were God-given. Whereas some have interpreted the Heiligenstadt Testament as a grandiose suicide note, there is much to recommend it, on the contrary, as an evocation of hope and compassion.

Perhaps it is plausible that only months earlier, such dark thoughts, tempered by cautious optimism, were somehow at play in the creation of his Second Symphony. But none of that is discernible in the florid, even carefree confections of his elegant B-flat Piano Sonata, Op. 22. And indeed, the forthrightness, largesse, and nobility of the D Major Symphony seem to belie as much, as well. But with the publication of the Sonata Quasi una Fantasia, Op. 27, No.2, also known as the "Moonlight" Sonata, only a month before the symphony's debut, something of his melancholy and emotional turmoil surfaced, ruffling the now placid, now violent surfaces of that work, which would eventually become one of his most popular.

Elsewhere, as the Napoleonic era took foot and ushered in the new century in the spirit of war, a coterie of armed conflicts was suddenly brought to a halt with the Treaty of Amiens. As wealthy merrymakers in powdered wigs and the emboldened new commoner sidled up to the daring new strains of the audacious young Beethoven, life went on. Though already celebrated among cognoscenti, Beethoven's music was still largely hearsay outside of Europe. In America, where Thomas Jefferson's romantic liaison with a slave girl had Washington aflutter in scandal, no one knew the music or much cared; the establishment of West Point Academy was far more newsworthy, as it echoed the military sentiments that ruled the day even from afar. It was the year, too, that saw the invention of photography, when British physicist Thomas Wedgwood produced the first crude, though ephemeral, image the world had ever known. It was a year that saw no particularly significant contributions to literature, though François Gerard completed his oddly melancholy and soon-to-be-renowned painting *Madame Recamier.*

It was into this environment that Beethoven's Second Symphony was born, and it gave way to both adulation and puzzlement. While the first movement charmed just about everyone, and the ensuing Larghetto enthralled all who heard it, the Finale fell on deaf ears—no pun intended!—and inspired the critical venom of those who found it disturbing, cacophonous, and wholly unintelligible.

First movement: Adagio molto; Allegro con brio

At first glance, the tempo indication of this first movement appears to beg the question of originality. As we have seen, Beethoven had already assigned the same tempo to the first movement of the First Symphony.

But that's where any similarity between the two ends. The opening salvo is a brusque, *fortissimo* dotted figure that the entire orchestra, given over to a single pitch, D, dispatches in unison. A brief consolation, yielded at once to the oboes, follows, only to be supplanted a few bars later by another descending dotted figure. No sooner does this stately introduction begin than Beethoven, introducing the theme to the violins, ornaments it in trills while hastening the pace in triplets.

Mind you, the character of this opening Adagio molto, with its persistent dotted rhythms and rich ornamentation, evokes a baroque compositional tradition, namely, the French overture. But unlike the conventional articulation of that regal form, Beethoven's version sets things firmly in triple rather than duple meter. The orchestration, too, is demonstrably more luxurious than the sparser configurations of the C Major Symphony, setting up at once an enriched dialogue between winds and strings that, as things develop, plays out in the body of meandering scale passages in thirty-second-notes. This gradual acceleration of pace is important in that it anticipates the manner in which Beethoven, in his later symphonies especially, would manipulate rhythm as a means of compressing time.

This point brings us to a particularly relevant issue, too, and one that was perhaps even more important in Beethoven's own day. How we as listeners experience the passage of time in a musical composition depends just as much on the temporal organization of the work itself as it does on our individual listening habits. The unfolding of a musical idea, no matter how abbreviated, does not occur in stasis or in a vacuum, but is a matter of *becoming*. While today our ears, long accustomed to the conventions of classical music, may perceive the development of a motivic fragment into something more expansive that also alters our perception of time (in that we relate to its variants in a new way each time we encounter it), the audiences of Beethoven's day may have reacted somewhat differently.

Indeed, post-Enlightenment Europe, embracing with fervor its new-found idealism, grasped for ways to express this abstraction in everyday language. The irreversible social changes brought about by the French Revolution reverberated in colorful metaphors, which favored nature imagery. People across the Continent spoke passionately of the passage of time as concomitant with progress, while vicissitudes of the spirit were extolled as a matter of secular thinking as much as religious. As the old order gave way to the new, change became popular in phrases that paid homage to it in powerful metaphors that only Nature herself could equal. Thus floods and winds, storms and torrents, streams and thunder became emblems not only of social upheaval, but of their relation to time. Just as a violent storm could alter a landscape in hours or an earthquake could devastate a land mass beyond recognition in the blink of an eye, so, too, could the forces of spiritual independence bring about a rupture within the cushy continuum that for so long had defined history as linear and cyclical. Time had now become a matter of perspective, as well as purposeful; it was no longer thought of as merely linear, but was viewed as eventful and thus as a work in progress en route to some greater goal.

So as Beethoven's Second made its debut, the very concept of time was changing, echoing society's burgeoning impatience and its increasing appetite for instant gratification. The accepted formalities of classical decorum, with its fetishization of reason, formal symmetry, and ornamentation, had suddenly become as anachronistic as they were superficial. Like unbridled adolescents trying to break from the authority of their parents, people hungered for a new kind of life experience, one that was more fulfilling, emotionally honest, and spiritually inspired.

If in Beethoven's music they found what they were looking for, it must have come as a revelation of overwhelming proportions. The huge and often violent dynamic contrasts, the abrupt and jarring rhythms that plowed forth with the power of an oncoming tsunami, and the unabashed lyrical ardor exploded the inherited expectations of its listeners. The experience of time, as articulated in tone, had been transformed from something reasonable and predictable to something explosive, edgy, and totally unexpected. To this end, Beethoven's music not only reflected, but also embodied his listeners' anxieties, as well as those of the world they had just collectively re-created.

Thus there is perhaps something especially emblematic about the Second Symphony's introduction, precisely because it makes a nod in the direction of its baroque ancestor. This immanent reference to the conventions of an older form colors the Adagio's relationship to the ensuing Allegro molto and makes the appearance of the latter all the more shocking. It is as if the Allegro molto's interjection, with its sunbursts of swift scales in the strings punctuated with reminders of the Adagio's opening dotted figure, was positioned to contradict the Old World's dying wish.

When a majestic yet fairly straightforward theme emerges in the clarinets and bassoons, something else vaguely French raises its Gallic head. It may not be a coincidence that something about this theme resembles the "Marseillaise," but the resemblance is only fleeting. A nervous, spitfire five-note fragment in sixteenth-notes, rising in *pianissimo* and separated by tense silences, reintroduces the Allegro molto's sinuous first theme and brings the exposition to a close.

The interplay between the strings and winds exploits this very fragment with unusual enthusiasm as the development presses on to the recapitulation and a vigorous coda. The concluding seven bars introduce a valiant yet also a humorous touch, in the deepest sense of the German word for it; "humor" in German signifies a good deal more than amusement and embraces something considerably darker. In these measures, Beethoven once again reintroduces the dotted motive of the Adagio's opening. In so doing, he harks back to the stylistic throwback it represents, thus demonstrating his compassion for the spirit of an earlier era.

Second movement: Larghetto

Though it was Mendelssohn whose famous piano works coined the phrase "Songs Without Words," much the same can be said of this stellar Larghetto. Surely one of Beethoven's most abundantly lyrical confections, this work has more to recommend it than its melodic enchantments. Even so, the Larghetto blossoms forth with a demeanor so tender as to betray its creator's most secret and most personal thoughts.

It is surprising that Beethoven declined to cast this sumptuous melody as a set of variations, as he often did in later works for the piano. Indeed, there is a remarkable similarity between the motivic events in this work and the variations that form the first movement of the A-flat

Piano Sonata, Op. 26. And years later, the finale of the E Major Piano Sonata, Op. 109, would likewise be a set of variations on a tune that bears a structural likeness to the Larghetto's songlike spin.

Instead, he initiates the movement with a fully fleshed-out eight-bar phrase, laying out the melody en route to its development in the context of traditional sonata form: exposition, development, and recapitulation. Even the key relations are perfectly in keeping with tradition: A major, which is the dominant of D major, is the key center.

But respect for formal tradition never compromised innovation in Beethoven's capable hands. After the violins, which carry the principal melody of the opening bars in a gentle four-note slope from E to C-sharp, thus establishing its prominence, Beethoven sees fit to repeat that melody. But the clarinets and bassoons, now dulcet and restrained, take over as if to reinforce the theme's ever-so-earnest sagacity.

This is a good place to introduce another concept of value, one that all listeners, no matter their level of musical understanding, can easily take for granted. I refer to the notion of *accompaniment*. Certainly, no one can argue that the generic, commonly understood sense of the word refers to the role of tones that linger quietly in the background as they lend harmonic support to the principal melody. Indeed, the melody may lie below, above, or even between these supportive figures. But the idea of accompaniment, in the full flower of its meaning, turns Freud's famous—if perhaps apocryphal—aphorism "Sometimes a cigar is just a cigar" into a gross oversimplification.

Indeed, there may be some truth to the assertion that there is no such thing as "accompaniment," insofar as the term demeans both the role and the substance of compositional activity. As we listen to a piece of music, particularly one as ostensibly pleasant and charming as the Larghetto of the Second Symphony, we are immediately pulled in, as it were, by the main melody. Wherever it lurks, and wherever it surfaces, our ears automatically follow. We are in effect ensorcelled by it. But above, below, and surrounding the main melody are other figures, which either complement or contradict it in the service of creating a single harmonious entity. These discrete figurations, the interplay of which is the fundamental definition of counterpoint, announce themselves in any number of ways: as motivic fragments, or repeated notes (pedal points), or individually crafted melodic strands, which contradict the direction or mood of the melody. Make no mistake: these figures are no less vital and richly configured than the melody that captures our attention so powerfully, sometimes to the exclusion of the equally important events at play in the so-called accompaniment.

In fact, if you listen very carefully and allow yourself to focus on these barely hidden contrapuntal threads, you will observe how vital they are to the composition's texture, and how richly configured, too. More often than not, these figures are the source of musical tension, excitement, and anticipation: even the reiteration of a single note can project a kind of melodic intent as it drives forward its more prominent neighbors atop its figurative shoulders. As you begin to play closer attention to these figures, you will find yourself in league not only with the intentions of composer, but with the interpretive values of the performer, as well.

Thus, when in the opening measures of the Larghetto the violins and violas migrate from the prosperity of the melody to a group of arpeggiated sixteenth-notes, their musical participation is no less valid; they have not suddenly gone on holiday! Even in a figure of this sort (often referred to as an *Alberti bass* in piano music), which breaks a single chord into its constituents, has purpose and direction. In the presence of such a figure, you might glean something more of its contextual role if you listen *through* it. Try to imagine it not as a single voice, that is, as a merely linear entity, but instead as two distinct voices at play and in tandem. As the lower notes of the figure interact with their upper neighbors, we begin to discern a dialogue between the two.

Poised in a more transparent dialogue, however, is the second theme, a charming dotted-note-motive theme given over to the upper registers of the violins and the middle registers of the clarinets and oboes. They toss the theme back and forth in an amiable rivalry, and then this new, all-too-brief gesture comes to a sudden halt, interrupted by a stern rhythmic salvo in a rousing *fortissimo*. Then, with a flourish of insistent pedal points resounded against a sequence of expressive arpeggios, Beethoven intensifies the material before returning to the principal theme.

Third movement: Scherzo: Allegro (CD Track 2)

Beethoven wasted no time in moving from the quasi-scherzo (né minuet) of the First Symphony to a full-fledged scherzo here. Its sparse orchestral texture, combined with its brevity, contributes significantly to its humor. There's a certain reductionism at work here, too; the entire piece is nothing if not a playful, even capricious dialogue where no one instrument or group of instruments is afforded the theme in its entirety. Instead, we are bombarded with abbreviated four-note fragments, which are continually passed from the strings to the woodwinds in a kind of cat-and-mouse game.

Beethoven humors us with the unusual construction of the ever-so-brief principal motive: the fourth note of the fragment, which occurs on a downbeat, falls precipitously by nearly two octaves from the pitch that precedes it (0:02). This always struck me as a likely source of inspiration for that the most recognized motivic fragment of Mendelssohn's incidental music to *A Midsummer Night's Dream*, where he paints in tone a donkey's neigh. We can only speculate what Beethoven had been reading at the time he was composing this scherzo!

Following a two-bar scale passage that veers off briefly into the remote key of B-flat, we hear something reminiscent of the principal theme of the first movement's Allegro con brio (0:24). That goes on for a scant ten bars, when once again our donkey guffaws his way to the surface (0:37).

The trio that follows is conventional enough, in that it respects the traditions of its form, yielding as it does to horn calls and a nod to bucolic reverie (1:52). The B section of the trio thrusts itself forward with an odd response to the distant horns, traversing an F-sharp major arpeggio in the style of a piano exercise (2:05). In my view, this is no accident. This short-lived but mischievous survey posits innocuous pleasure against minimal pain, suggesting that diligence and study will be amply rewarded so long as decorum is respected.

Fourth movement: Allegro molto

The tumultuous peculiarity of the opening of this tightly woven Allegro molto led Hector Berlioz to refer to it as a "second scherzo in double time." Though it is not technically a scherzo at all, there is nonetheless something about this movement's cheekiness and good humor that supports that notion. And besides, who wants to argue with Berlioz?

Just as in the forgoing scherzo, Beethoven again puts an exceptionally large interval to work, dropping suddenly off the precipice of a high G in the flutes and violins to a bumptious C-sharp an octave and half below, intensifying the moment with a trill and a sforzando. A tenuous second theme in the form of only five ascending notes in stepwise motion surfaces unceremoniously in the cellos and violins, only to be usurped a few moments later by the clarinets and bassoons.

Rising to prominence throughout the movement is the playful, even capricious two-note, short-to-long motive that begins the movement. Its character is that of an appoggiatura, or "leaning" note, wherein a dissonant pitch (one that does not belong to the prevailing key or harmony) "leans into" its subsequent neighbor. Here the distance between them is only a half step; the narrow proximity of the two notes yields something of a relentless, insistent patina. Indeed, Beethoven puts the figure to work as a kind of humorous commentary, as if it were thumbing its motivic nose at the other themes. This figure, which Beethoven distributes effortlessly between the strings and woodwinds, is in fact the fundamental germ that drives the work along rhythmically and lends itself to the restless, if puckish, climate that informs it. The last six bars are devoted almost entirely to one pitch, the tonic D, which brings this cheerful Allegro to its resounding close.

Symphony No. 3 in E-flat Major, Op. 55 ("Eroica")

2 Flutes, 2 Oboes, 2 Clarinets (B-flat),
2 Bassoons, 3 Horns (E-flat and C), 2 Trumpets
(E-flat and C), Timpani, Violins I and II, Violas,
Cellos, Basses

Composed between 1802 and 1804

First performance in Vienna, December 1804,
at the home of Prince von Lobkowitz; first public
performance at Theater-an-der-Wien, April 7, 1805

Dedicated to Prince Franz Joseph von Lobkowitz

First movement: Allegro con brio
Second movement: Marcia funebre: Adagio assai
Third movement: Scherzo; Allegro vivace
Fourth movement: Finale: Allegro molto; Poco andante

This landmark work, which inaugurated Beethoven's so-called "heroic period," remains to this day one of the most widely discussed and debated of all his compositions. It is surrounded by popular myth, the most celebrated of which is its relation to Napoleon, to whom Beethoven had originally dedicated it. But, as legend goes, when Napoleon named himself emperor, a disillusioned Beethoven ripped up the title page and never looked back. The inscription was replaced with a cynical nod, the intent of which was aimed at power more than Napoleon per se. Thus on the title page, Beethoven's words, "Composed to celebrate the memory of a great man," were more than a sentimental echo or the expression of disappointment, but a slap in the face of what until then had been a symbol of revolutionary expectation.

Beethoven's "heroic period" refers to a style of composition that took off in new directions, which, though nowhere near as radical as some believe, challenged the aesthetics, if not the rules, of conventional classicism. Here, at the risk of compromising classical decorum, Beethoven frequently exploited increasingly startling contrasts, pungent harmonies, and explosive, even compulsive rhythms. If there was indeed an underlying, extramusical context, it became a moot point, as the music itself embodied a kind of internecine debate that took place among its various elements, as if they were in a kind of heightened competition with each other.

First movement: Allegro con brio (CD Track 3)

That Beethoven chose to frame a work of such uncompromising intensity as this Allegro con brio in triple time—that is, the same metrical organization into three beats per bar as a minuet, a waltz, or the famous scherzi that became nearly synonymous with the mention of his name—is in itself extraordinary. And yet, Beethoven uses this meter as a means to develop an abundance of truncated themes, nearly all of which are defined by their fragmentary status as opposed to their periodic development.

Everything about this movement defies expectation. The addition of a third horn to the symphonic texture, though innovative, was more likely a consequence of Beethoven's overall compositional strategy. The woodwinds in this symphony (including the horns, which were at that time considered part of the woodwind section) boast a role of greater prominence and structural necessity, as opposed to supportive or imitative.

Two gigantic E-flat chords, separated by two quarter-rests, pulsate in full *forte* and are played by the entire orchestra in anticipation of the principal theme (0:00). The entry of that theme in the cellos is surprising not only for its dynamic reduction from *forte* to *piano*, but also for its pithy economy (0:04). But it is merely a fragment, an arpeggiated survey of a simple E-flat triad. The serenity of the figure, accompanied by a placid group of eighth-notes assigned to the violins, is disturbed by the introduction of a C-sharp, the sixth degree of the E-flat scale raised by a half step (0:09). Its presence, though only momentary, suggests uncertainty, a climate supported by the syncopated pedal point on G set forth at the same time by the first violins.

Now it's the woodwinds' turn. Their assumption of the principal theme sets the record straight, so to speak, restoring stability following that earlier, momentary flight to a foreign pitch (0:20). A hemiola-rich second motive proffers itself in the tonic, rather than dominant, key, thus prolonging the sense of anticipation firmly established by the material of the opening bars. This motive, again a fragment on the order of a transitional passage rather than a distended periodic melody, is offset by sforzandos imposed on every other beat (0:30). The figure also projects the same distended triadic attitude of the opening, ascends with uncommon vigor, and suggests a certain discomfort with itself. But its struggle pays off, and just as we might have expected a lavish new second period to begin, Beethoven introduces still another motivic fragment, this time a lyrical, descending three-note figure passed first among the flutes, oboes, and clarinets, and then over to the violins (0:59).

A brief "galloping" motive is next to put in an appearance in this rich roster of abbreviated themes (1:25) while Beethoven's continuous imposition of sforzandos on weak beats lends to the work an unusual sense of urgency. Still centered in the tonic key, without any foreseeable change, the exposition bears witness to yet another fragment, this time a plaintive whisper in *piano* (1:48). The subtle chromatic, stepwise motion that infiltrates it gives up its domain to the imminent machismo of the ensuing theme, which at some eighty-five bars into the piece—an unusually long time in the household of classical-era sonata form—establishes the dominant.

Let's step back now and take a moment to look at what all this activity means in the larger scheme of things. The nature metaphors of the early nineteenth century notwithstanding, there is a great deal about the "Eroica" Symphony that celebrates complexity, that would make of it a poster child for upheaval and change in post-revolutionary Europe. But to do so only demeans the abundance of its ideas. Rather, with its tumble of thematic fragments, its prolongation of tension through fragmentation, its lengthy development that sets forth yet new themes and rhythms, and its extended coda, what really distinguishes this Allegro is its disposition toward the passage of time. Its monumentality as a whole is one thing, but the sheer abundance of musical data, which most certainly overwhelmed contemporary ears, is quite another.

Things seem to press forward with uncommon urgency while the smallest motivic details, such as we have just examined, become objects of compositional scrutiny and relentless development. From the lyrical passivity of the all-too-brief opening theme to the nearly belligerent collective into which the array of motives eventually coalesces, our understanding of time is altered. What had been so easily discernible and even pleasant in his earlier symphonies and, indeed, in the music of his predecessors—namely the orderly unfolding of a few key themes tidily dispatched en route to their dénouement—in the "Eroica" assume a new and perhaps more serious role. The introduction of so much new material so meticulously manipulated and deftly integrated points again to the political realities of the age, without making any overt or explicit symbolic reference; there are no clear-cut allusions, for example, either rhythmic or harmonic, to the sound of cannons or to indigenous patriotic songs. Rather, it is the overcoming of this material in the face of so many possibilities, and potential adversities, that Beethoven broke new ground. To be sure, this is not an entirely musical phenomenon, but here it is informed by a larger aesthetic that saw in such "overcoming" an opportunity for a work of art to engage all men in a new vocabulary of thought and spirit.

In this climate of unprecedented artistic complexity, where the integrity of the whole depended like never before on the character and organization of the smallest motivic particles (harking back, perhaps, to the compositional principles of the baroque but within in an expanded technical and historical context), the average listeners benefited from the confidence that such challenging music inspired in them. Compelled in its presence to make sense of its myriad parts and its fast-moving and ever-changing rhythms, listeners of Beethoven's day, just like listeners today, were engrossed by the music's dense tapestry of juxtaposed motives, themes, and counterpoint. The destiny of those elements held them enthralled as it engaged them intellectually and emotionally to stay afloat in the wash of musical information. The very idea of "order" took on an entirely new and perhaps metaphorical meaning.

Nowhere is this more obvious than in the munificent development section (3:24), which not only cooks the themes already introduced in the exposition, but extends them to nearly 250 bars. So vast is the network of thematic relationships that our experience of time, rather than being suspended or slowed down, is just the opposite. The flurry of compositional activity, informed by the intensification of every one of the extant themes, flatters our ability to listen to music for its cumulative power. Musical events barrel forth at a furious pace. Those very elements tumble forward with exhilarating panache; we feel as if time has been accelerated and moved forward, like a thousand new suns and planets that, riding astride a beam of light from a distant galaxy eons old, have just become visible. In the midst of all this grandeur, and following a sequence of unusually dissonant syncopations (6:18), Beethoven offers a wholly new theme, at once lyrical and effusive, but also oddly melancholy (6:40).

That said, the recapitulation, which is normally an occasion for the restatement of materials introduced by the exposition, offers a particularly fascinating innovation, one not without consequences. Here, at its onset, tonic and dominant are combined in tandem, the horns enveloping the former tonality while the strings avail themselves of the latter (9:34). Naturally, this creates an unusually effective, even ethereal, environment. This moment was so disturbing to trained as well as amateur ears of Beethoven's time that the publisher, convinced it was a misprint, smoothed it all over and rewrote it. Fortunately, it wasn't at all long before that publisher's presumptuousness in the face of genius was roundly condemned, and he was compelled to restore Beethoven's explicit intentions.

The coda of this symphony belies its traditional definition as something more or less tacked on, a kind of summing up of the recurring themes (13:16). Here it presumes to become a critique of all that has gone before it and, to a certain extent, of what is to follow. There is also a certain reductionism at work here; hairpin crescendos dovetail with increasing frequency, modifying the material, while the horns are configured prominently and attract attention. The earlier "galloping" motive, too, takes center stage as the strings pit it against the principal theme and then are propelled forward in the context of an ongoing crescendo (15:16). The strings vibrate in tremolos while the horns and trumpets take over the now familiar principal theme of the opening. Elsewhere, the timpani lend their bulbous support from below and leave us with the impression that all is not over, even as the work comes to a close. After all that activity, the deed, it seems to say, is not yet done; there is meaning, both musical (for its stoic anticipation of what is about to be) and symbolic (for what so many contradictory elements suggest when in play simultaneously with each other), that goes well beyond the confines of bar lines, the movement itself, and indeed the entire piece.

Second movement: Marcia funebre; Adagio assai

This sorrowful elegy, a lugubrious march in C minor, so simple in design yet powerful in its effect, embodies its sorrows with considerable austerity. While its mood is somber, there is nothing about either its form or content that in any way compromises its intensity.

Accompanying the principal melody, a continuous pulsation of thirty-second-note triplets, given over to the second violins, violas, and cellos as the work gets under way, becomes a prescient evocation of a funeral procession. This figure, which Brahms would use in a nearly identical manner decades later in the Intermezzo of his F minor piano sonata, represents the distant rumblings of drums in the mournful procession. The reassignment of this bit of itinerant melancholia to a lone oboe only eight bars into the movement serves to emphasize a sense of isolation that, in musical terms, is oddly existential. A brief respite, which at first appears to auger in the relative major of E-flat, interrupts and gives pause for hope. But this, too, is abruptly interrupted by a rhetorical flourish of a dotted figure in *forte*. The melody is thrown again to the violins, and back yet again to an oboe and flute.

Then, without warning, the gloomy countenance of the opening is rendered transparent by a new idea in C major. Here again, intonatsiia goes to work for attentive listeners, compelling them to feel the disposition of the space in between these two distinct tonal regions. The sudden juxtaposition of minor and major keys is startling even to the most naive ears, as the latter suggests that all is not lost, that even in the face of adversity, there is hope. Like the sun peering out from behind a dark cloud, the music takes on a wholly new and consoling personality. Indeed, this new section reinvents the ominous triplets of the opening with another species of triplet. But this figure, aside from being in a major key, moves at a slower pace and is notated as sixteenth, not thirty-second notes. An oboe and flute sing out above in an all-too-brief tender duet, before being joined by a bassoon, and then the entire orchestra (tutti). The strings get their way, too, with this infusion of optimism in the midst of tragedy. A succession of weighty dominant chords precedes a somewhat playful figure of articulated duplets, cut from the whole cloth of the preceding triplets; the third note of each triplet group is replaced by a sixteenth-rest. A monumental crescendo in the final bars of this section imparts a certain fearlessness as it hemorrhages into a restatement of the original theme.

As if to make another point that would contradict any idea of the existential, Beethoven launches into a fugue that insists on order, not chaos; he demands meaning in a universe that he refuses to accept as being devoid of it. As the fugato winds down, the first violins scream out in repeated notes on a high D and E-flat, while an anxiety-rich motive swells up above and below in the strings and woodwinds. Then suddenly, the texture thins out; the principal theme returns briefly in the first violins, then alights, and finally pauses on a single A-flat. The anticipatory silence is at once palpable and eerie. Then, in a measure of defiance, Beethoven pays tribute to the basses, which yield their dark sonorities in a tense delivery of closely aligned triplets as the trumpets blare forth overhead in fanfare, summoning the departed spirits as surely as Mozart's Stone Guest summoned Don Juan to hell. The transitional second theme that in the opening gave us a short-lived glimpse of E-flat major now assumes a new burnished ardor and penetrating warmth.

It isn't long before we hear again the funeral theme and the thirty-second-note triplets, the former carried by the flutes, and the latter exclusively by the strings. However, this time there is a certain urgency, even a militant forthrightness about them. Following this is a very odd figure indeed: a languid but syncopated dialogue between the first and second violins provides a moment of touching lyricism in the midst of so much grief, and it leads us into the coda. This brief interlude is introduced by a four-bar roundabout of two notes, A-flat and C, that evokes the ticking of a clock. It is a rather apparent symbolic nod toward the idea of time having run out. And indeed it has: as the orchestral texture thins out, we hear only a quiescent trace of the original theme, played sotto voce by the first violins against a sparse bass pizzicato.

Third movement: Scherzo; Allegro vivace

The mercurial opening of this subtle scherzo is no joke, but a breezy whirlwind that angles upward, in stepwise motion, in *pianissimo* and staccato. The mood is indeed vivacious, even restless. But the puckish interplay of the first theme, tossed causally from the violins to the oboes, and then to the flutes, gives notice that all the sorrow expressed by the funeral march has vanished; life goes on.

This scherzo is all aflutter; it flies off the page and into space with such quixotic abandon that we are hardly aware of what lends it its integrity. To be sure, the tightly woven rhythm that is responsible for just that consists of three quarter-beats per bar. These move along so rapidly that they are best counted (and conducted) as one beat, that is, as a single gesture.

The discreet hush of the opening blossoms into a resounding *fortissimo*, a rustic revelry that ushers in the bucolic horn calls of the trio that follows. But then, as if to thumb his nose at the equestrian and fox-hunting pastimes of the aristocracy, to whom such bucolic harmonies nearly always point, Beethoven disrupts the rhythm with four bars in duple, rather than triple, time. A joke? Maybe so!

Fourth movement: Finale: Allegro molto

Whatever it is that, for two hundred years, has inspired the endearment and affection that this Finale so richly deserves may remain a mystery. The breadth of Beethoven's imagination, revealing itself here in a set of variations on the flimsiest skeleton of a tune, is remarkable enough in its own right. Certainly, it would be challenging enough to decipher in detail, and with the authority of scholarship, every ineluctable moment as the work develops. To be sure, professional musicians, especially young conductors learning the "Eroica" for the first time, would be well advised to survey every analysis they possibly can.

And yet for all that, what can define, or even displace our perception of the nobility and authentic heroism, which it conveys so powerfully and unmistakably? Is our experience of this imperial finale, which takes the most insignificant thematic kernel and turns it into something so wholly humane and universal, something extramusical that we merely imagine and that is not implicit to the music itself?

The answer is yes, in technical categories. And that's precisely where we come up against a lingering problem for both musical aesthetics and philosophy. And perhaps in the final analysis (no pun intended!), whether it is or it isn't extramusical doesn't really matter. One would either have to be inhuman or deaf from birth to not come away from the "Eroica," and from this movement in particular, unmoved and indifferent to the nobility of its character and the fundaments of its message, which, given the display of mastery over form and content, yet again suggests the rallying cry of the age—to wit, overcoming adversity.

The movement begins with a grand flourish. The strings sally forth with an impetuous announcement, a vigorous descent of running sixteenth-notes. The principal theme, which is so sparse that its first half boasts only two notes, E-flat and B-flat spread out over four bars and separated by rests, introduces itself. This melody, which is the basis for a set of variations to follow, continues for yet another four bars, wherein Beethoven slightly accelerates its pace. Its mood is coy, as if whoever or whatever was behind it was merely toying with its observer.

This bare-bones melody was hardly new when Beethoven used it here. Evidently one of his favorite thematic postulates, he had worked it into several earlier compositions, including *The Creatures of Prometheus*, a contradance, and a piano work, *Variations on a Theme from Prometheus*, Op. 33. While the strings are given a hefty share of the work here, sporting their material with virtuosic fervor, the woodwinds—flutes, oboes, bassoons, clarinets, and horns, too—obtain to a special quality absent from the First and Second symphonies. Indeed, in the "Eroica," and nowhere more so than in this Finale, their role is perhaps less "coloristic" and supportive than it is functional. With the introduction of a cheerful new theme in the third variation, the woodwinds enter into a dialogue with each other and the work suddenly takes on the character of a chamber concerto. But no sooner do the strings move in moments later to reassert their rights to this charming tune than the oboes, in hot pursuit, reappear and resume their guardianship.

Nowhere has Beethoven more ably proven that variations on a theme are a good deal more than the sum of their parts. For all the immanent activity that makes of this Finale something as efflorescent as it is ambitious, there is not a single wasted moment. It is as if, in its zeal to lead us on to some greater goal or musical conclusion, the work has grown wings and takes flight. No compositional device is too good for it, or goes unused, so long as it serves a useful, but moreover, an honest purpose. To that end, Beethoven manipulates the principal themes into an energetic but tightly woven fugato. Just in case anyone is confused by that fugue-like term, it means exactly that: fugue-like. Motivic fragments and melodies, which are the very substance of counterpoint (the linear combination of two or more melodies), tumble forth in succession, and in imitation of each other, without taking over entirely. In spite of its novelty as a means to develop extant musical material, a fugato is a localized phenomenon that occurs in a larger but unrelated form, in this case a set of variations. It neither informs nor defines the overall structure of the work it modifies, as it most certainly would were the prevailing form in fact and strictly a fugue.

But in this movement, a fugato is just one compositional device among many. Beethoven clearly had a very good time with this Finale, in that it allowed him to show off every trick in his compositional arsenal. And speaking of arsenal, a less than strident but aggressive dotted rhythm empowers the new melodic fragment that follows. Its swagger and purposefulness are suggestive of a military march and are played by the full orchestra in *forte*.

Few composers could express resignation more effectively than Beethoven, and he does so again in the final variation. Changing the tempo to *poco andante*, this lyrical variant projects a melodic attitude that is only loosely based on the original theme that informs it. The playful impetuosity of the foregoing variations is set aside in favor of what strikes us as an oddly melancholy final commentary. Distributed again amid the woodwinds in a dulcet dialogue, its ambiance, at once world-weary and somber, betrays an uncanny calm born of fortitude. This in turn moves into a new element, where a rotating compliment of triplets, played by the clarinets, is overshadowed by still another melodic variant that pulsates languidly in the first violins.

The triplets figure, now grown relentless and given over to the strings, and firmly buttressed by the timpani, intensifies until, surprisingly, the scale-like flourish of the Finale's opening returns, but this time much faster: Beethoven explicitly demands *presto*. This is yet another incidence where motivic material, reintroduced and recast in a new context, alters, accelerates, and manipulates our experience of time. And while our ears may have grown accustomed to as much thanks to repeated listening to this famous warhorse, the listeners of Beethoven's day had no such advantage.

Given its artful inventiveness and the innumerable elements of surprise that populate every corner of this music, one can only guess what effect it had on early nineteenth-century audiences. In a society free of electronics and mass communication, where horse-drawn carriages and walking determined the languid everyday rhythms of life, the abundance of activity and events embodied within the "Eroica" were likely overwhelming. After all, it was a great deal of information, albeit of an abstract nature, to absorb in just under an hour. In the minds of the befrock-coated bourgeoisie, the question was obvious: How can so much happen in so short a time, yet be presented so clearly, concisely, and purposefully? It hardly seemed possible, yet there it was, in symphonic form. Was such drive and cumulative energy likewise possible in other disciplines, including science? And what did it all mean for progress?

This smorgasbord of compositional data was in itself a critique of human potential, providing a means to measure, in aesthetic as much as in social categories, what energy and accomplishment were all about.

But we need not compare our listening habits with that of our ancestors; today our expectations have hardly been compromised by familiarity, thanks to the originality and complexity of the music itself.

Great art, which aspires to autonomy, has seen to that. On the contrary, with each subsequent hearing we are continually surprised by elements we may not have detected in previous encounters but that were already embedded within the musical text—waiting to be discovered.

That is a particularly useful thing to consider with each successive hearing: What strikes us as unusual or new about the music this time that did not the last? Each encounter with this symphony, or any great work of art, ought remain fresh and open to new possibilities. Just as a responsible and artistically gifted musician strives to bring out something new in each performance and rejects any notion of playing by rote in rigid duplication of earlier readings, so we, as listeners, must continually reinvent our experience of musical values and potential. Again, we are reminded, as Roland Barthes opined, to inscribe ourselves in the work, as if we were composing it while it unfolds before us.

This is intonatsiia once more rearing its useful and significant head. We are now beginning to listen outside the box, as it were, but also *inside* it. We cannot reproduce the contextual environment of nineteenth-century listeners, as we live in a world of our own making very different than that of so many generations ago. But in spite of that, something within the music—its truth content, if you will—reveals itself and allows us a glimpse into authenticity preserved in tone and rhythm, an authenticity as much imbued with the spirit and letter of Beethoven's day as much as our own. We are dialectically engaged with this music, observing it objectively as we simultaneously scrutinize ourselves in relation to it, yet without callously dismissing our subjective feelings, either. It may be that the most useful and rewarding idea, for sophisticated listeners who may not be able to engross themselves in theoretical purviews, is to embrace every moment of musical experience as an eminently adequate measure of learning and understanding.

And so, as the "Eroica" Symphony concludes on a bright and optimistic series of prolonged E-flat chords, we, too, emboldened by that optimism, look forward to hearing it again, and again—and again.

Symphony No. 4
in B-flat Major, Op. 60

Flute, 2 Oboes, 2 Clarinets (B-flat), 2 Bassoons,
2 Horns (B-flat, E-flat), 2 Trumpets (B-flat, E-flat),
Timpani, Violins I and II, Violas, Cellos, Basses

Composed 1806

First performance March 1807 at the home of
Prince Lobkowitz, Vienna

Dedicated to Count Franz von Oppersdorf

First movement: Adagio; Allegro vivace
Second movement: Adagio
Third movement: Allegro vivace
Fourth movement: Allegro, ma non troppo

The quiescent strains of this robust symphonic reverie were nothing if not a provision of sanctuary for a war-weary world. While French forces busied themselves conquering Berlin and Warsaw and confronting the Russians, the no less bellicose British were firebombing Copenhagen, for no other reason than to compel their cooperation against Napoleon. In faraway America, scandal once again rocked the nation, just as it still does, when Vice President Aaron Burr was accused, then acquitted, of conspiracy and treason. The French painter Ingres, whose meticulous eye brought a new elegance to representative portraiture, had just completed another masterpiece, *Madame Rivière*.

Against this backdrop, the Fourth Symphony, an oasis of lyrical restraint and fantasy, made its debut. Its musical stature, though certainly on par with the shattering innovations of the "Eroica" on one side, and the monumental Fifth Symphony on the other, has at times been challenged by those who see in it something less "revolutionary" than either of its sister works.

Its form and content, though conventional, in no way compromise Beethoven's outspoken compositional vocabulary. The Adagio moves by gracefully as it gives voice to one memorable melody after another, and the composer's symphonic form of favor, the scherzo, is accorded its usual place in the symphonic hierarchy

Indeed, there is something conservative, even retroactive, about this symphony, which is not to suggest by any means that it is unimaginative. On the contrary, in revisiting the conventional forms and ideational strategies that influenced him, Beethoven reinvents them. On the heels of the "Eroica" Symphony, he had nothing to prove, but only to express. Though Beethoven confessed, some years in advance of composing the Third Symphony, that he aimed to change the paradigm of composition, here his authority is assured. The Fourth offers no political capital, either explicit or implied; no rounds of militaristic rhythms or warlike drums (a long but quiet passage of timpani in the first movement notwithstanding) come into play. It would be difficult for anyone to invest political capital in this work; its musical independence, divorced from the burden of wholly subjective but extramusical ideals (at least on the composer's part), allows it to satisfy its own concept.

This is not to say, mind you, that Beethoven turned a cold shoulder to musical metaphor and was indifferent to the associative imagery his music inspired in others as well as in himself. But it seems that in this piece, he made no special effort to suggest, by instrumental and compositional means, anything beyond purely musical meaning.

We may wonder if Beethoven, who was vacationing at a countryside estate at the time of its composition, was inspired in some way by the natural beauty of his environment. At the same time, the Fifth Symphony, which would again give expression to defiance and invoke so much political speculation, was well under way; he had already begun sketching it. The inherent contradictions posed by these two works in relation to each other could not have escaped him. One thing is certain: the results bore uncommon fruit, and we are its beneficiaries.

In spite of its overall acceptance at the time, with few detractors, the Fourth Symphony inspired controversy in some unexpected quarters. Indeed, the twenty-year-old composer and critic Carl Maria von Weber, whose opera *Der Freischütz* and unusually provocative piano sonatas would later endow him with celebrity of his own, was presumptuous and vicious in equal measure. His Teutonic fangs dripping with venom over the alleged inadequacies of the Fourth Symphony, Weber accused his eminent colleague of a lack of imagination. The work, he opined, "is full of short, disjointed, unconnected ideas which move along at the rate of three or four notes per quarter of an hour . . . it capers about like a wild goat to execute the no-ideas of Mr. Composer."

First movement: Adagio; Allegro vivace

The mysterious aura that informs the introductory Adagio is made all the more so by the dark murmurings of the bass and the suggestion of a minor tonality. In lowering, within the first few measures, both the sixth and third degrees of the B-flat scale (G to G-flat, and D to D-flat), Beethoven engenders a certain disquiet. The mood is tense and prescient; the stage has been set. The strings and woodwinds, in a thin but timorous presentation of the initial theme, lie in wait for something more definitive. Things become even more tenuous, but exciting, as a sudden but forceful crescendo on four A-naturals (the penultimate pitch, or "leading tone" that abuts the tonic B-flat) leads into the Allegro vivace.

Here, in anticipation of the principal theme of this section (a boisterous arpeggiation of four eighth-notes played by the strings and woodwinds over four bars), a rush of sixteenths angle swiftly upward as if to announce the arrival of something important. The mood has changed entirely; things are now redolent with the composer's customary optimism. The strings then set in motion a nervous trill spelled out in eighth-notes, only to be disrupted by a transitional passage set ablaze by our aforementioned musical friend the hemiola. A flute, oboe, and bassoon then parry with a new theme that is once again suggestive of bucolic charms. A lyrical fragment in quarter-notes follows and is given additional prominence by a clarinet and bassoon playing in tandem.

This is a good place to draw attention to the pervasive nature imagery in Beethoven's symphonies and, in fact, in every musical genre he wrote for. While it presents no particular problems for our listening apparatus and is easily recognizable even to untrained ears, its role and value to the music, and our experience of it, cannot be underestimated. More often than not these countryside references—to hunting, to fauna, to the weather—are codified by the woodwinds and couched in successive intervals of thirds and sixths. But they play such an enormously vital role in the music that to dismiss them as merely Beethovenian truisms would be ludicrous. Their role, as symbolic as it is functional, informs the substance as well as the musical trajectory; it clues us in on where things are headed. And as we shall see, Beethoven cultivates this to an extraordinary degree just a few years later in the Sixth ("Pastoral") Symphony.

The ensuing development puts to work all the foregoing elements, combining them in succession, as to be expected. But with the restatement of the principal thematic material in the recapitulation, they take on a brighter, more courageous, and uninhibited persona. A string of half-notes crescendos mightily over twelve bars en route to a stirring and conclusive coda.

Second movement: Adagio (CD Track 4)

As this delicious symphonic song extends itself outward for some twelve minutes, we are struck by the projection of a melodic "attitude" at virtually every turn. No strand of the counterpoint serves merely to support or imitate its neighbors; each is instead given over to detailed articulation. The first violins serve the tender opening theme, so warm and endearing, over a delicate dotted figure ratified by the second fiddles. The theme is simultaneously echoed in reverse by the violas, thus further enriching the musical scenery. Even the timpani accede to a unique role here in pulsating rhythms that are more lyrical in their shapeliness than they are percussive (1:00).

The Adagio is in the key of E-flat, which is to say, the subdominant of B-flat. While this may seem relatively unimportant, it has its place; built on the fourth degree of the scale, the subdominant exerts a subtle effect on our listening, that is, on the way in which we relate to one tonal field in juxtaposition with another.

A flute and oboe assume the principal melody early on (1:08), though not for long. The violins and flute, joining forces, introduce an ardent new fragment (2:01), accompanied by a particularly broad array of arpeggios in the strings. It's a somber and majestic moment to which a lone clarinet briefly responds with a haunting interjection that seems to emerge imperceptibly out of the larger texture (2:50). The violins, enchanted by that reedy instrument, plant their own seed in a languid succession of truncated triplets; a sixteenth-rest replaces one note of each triplet, thus giving the impression of duplets (3:03). As these alight and fall in a slow descent, the clarinet sings out.

A fluid string of thirty-second-notes, which proceed in a stately and unhurried manner in the larger context of a tempo adagio, are tossed between the violins and violas, while the basses, taking up the dotted rhythm, tremble below like heartbeats (3:44). Following a bellowing crescendo that modifies a steep succession of the now familiar dotted rhythm (4:10), from the low bass to the high flute, the principal melody returns. But now it is elaborated with slow-moving turns and flourishes (4:37) that prolong its refrain. A lone flute and a clarinet position themselves to present a final statement of the main theme, now reduced and encapsulated in only two bars (10:41). This leads to a charming though conclusive dialogue among the strings and woodwinds (10:59); a solo clarinet and flute, chirping like birds and heard in relief (11:04) give up their abbreviated solo interludes to the strings, which bring the movement to its triumphant *fortissimo* end.

Third movement: Scherzo: Allegro vivace

Had some clever publisher ever given this movement a name, it might well have been "Disruption." In effect, disruption is what it's all about: disruption of the prevailing mood, disruption of the normal rhythmic impetus of a scherzo, and disruption of metrical accentuation. Here, Beethoven converts three beats per bar into a perceptible two, but not entirely by means of hemiola. Instead, he draws slurs over two adjoining notes (long to short values) in each bar, then separates each microscopic duplet one from the other with a rest. This in turn effectively decimates the metrical conclusions that three beats per bar would normally have reached. What we experience in consequence is a kind of headlong rush toward stability, like an annoying hiccup in search of a longer breath.

Availing itself of these oddly out of sync syncopations, the flutes and strings become playful interlocutors, passing the articulated duplets back and forth to each other as in a game.

The trio is a lighter confection than what we have come to expect in Beethoven. Though the oboe carries its smile of a melody, its instrumental properties in combination with the registration convey an ambiance at once airy and serene. Meanwhile, a short and somewhat mischievous figure played by the violins edges things forward, culminating in a measured yet pervasive trill carried in unison by the strings. Just as the trio comes to a close, the timpani make an unexpected entrance and lend a bellicose but darker presence to the proceedings.

Fourth movement: Allegro ma non troppo

Exuberance and joy are the national anthem of this spirited Allegro ma non troppo. But there is a certain irony at work in this piece. If the new spirit of fraternal co operation and unity that defined the composer's era is anywhere present in music, it is certainly here, if only by virtue of what at first seems to be the democratic distribution of motivic materials. Every instrument gets to speak its mind in this movement, at least for a little while. But, to paraphrase George Orwell's famous dictum, "Some instruments are more equal than others." In this case, the strings, and the first violins in particular, take on the character of a bully at times, refusing to let anyone else get a word in edgewise.

A blistering run of sixteenth-notes inaugurates this movement, and they go on to infiltrate most of it with brusque determination. But they also act as a catalyst of sorts for a number of melodic fragments, which emerge out of them and come into their own. Indeed, only twelve bars into the piece, the first violins take up a broad descending motive, only four bars long, that is almost immediately picked up and elaborated by the flutes. The oboes, not to be outdone, provide some repose with a spacious theme of their own, accompanied by a stream of running triplets, which diminish the tension of the foregoing sixteenths, in the clarinets. Then, like a rude pugilist thumbing his fist at an opponent in an effort to capture his attention, a gang of four sforzandos, abruptly accentuated on both the first and second beats, distribute themselves in dialogue between the strings and woodwinds, while the timpani put in their two cents, too, on the second beat.

The pent-up energy here is as astonishing for its breadth as it is compulsive in execution. There is forthrightness at play, a certain unwillingness of the energy to compromise itself to anything that would threaten to attenuate it. The strings, to which the bulk of that kinetic energy are given, simply won't take no for an answer: they react to any new idea set forth by the woodwinds, no matter how charming, with the unforgiving imposition of someone determined to have the last word.

In the concluding moments of this breathless edifice, the first violins resign their authority and are left on their own to bleat out, in a single unaccompanied line, one final, melancholy regret. It's as if they had just confessed to being a very bad boy indeed. As if to rub it in, a bassoon blurts out four descending eighth-notes in weepy conciliation, only to be apologetically imitated by the second violins and violas. But then, of course, not to roll away in limpid defeat, the cellos, violas, and bassoon reiterate the impetuous calling card of belligerent sixteenths, this time a headlong downward rush toward the final three chords, which issue their definitive edict with force and gusto. Looks as if the violins, having at last convinced their instrumental brethren of the rightness of their position, get the last word, after all.

Symphony No. 5 in C Minor, Op. 67

Piccolo, 2 Flutes, 2 Oboes, 2 Clarinets (B-flat, C), Contrabassoon, 2 Horns, 2 Trumpets, Alto Trombone, Tenor Trombone, Bass Trombone, Timpani, Violins I and II, Violas, Cellos, Basses

Composed 1806–7

First performance: Theater-an-der-Wien, Vienna, December 22, 1808

Dedicated to Prince von Lobkowitz and Count Razumovsky

First movement: Allegro con brio
Second movement: Andante con moto
Third movement: Allegro
Fourth movement: Allegro

The year 1808 was an exceptionally busy time for Beethoven, who was not yet forty years old. As Russian forces marched into Finland, as if that country hadn't enough trouble, and while just about everyone was declaring war on an increasingly unpopular France, Beethoven was showered in a mixture of accolades and derision. This same year, 1808, that saw the debut of the Fifth Symphony, also bore witness to the first performances of the composer's fourth piano concerto and the no-less-grand Sixth ("Pastoral") Symphony. Such celebratory fervor did not leave him immune from criticism. Indeed, his introduction of piccolos and trombones into the symphonic texture of the Fifth upset more than one prominent critic, including Louis Spohr, who was also a prolific composer of innocuous songs and rather charming chamber music, and who found the innovation "disreputable."

Today Spohr's pronouncement sounds as shrill as it does naïve. What he failed to observe, or worse, deliberately declined to acknowledge, is that in formal categories, the Fifth Symphony is utterly conventional. There is no radical departure from sonata form, or periodic phrasing, or even the laws of harmonic progression. Nor is there any particular indictment of counterpoint or even the aesthetics of his day. Instead, Beethoven again demonstrates his mastery in ways that disavow any dereliction of compositional duty or indulgence for the sake of novel effect.

As we have already pointed out, his musical domicile was that of a composer determined to imaginatively reinvent and invigorate established musical forms, but from a fresh and thoroughly uncorrupted perspective. His objective was not to write music for the pleasure of the aristocracy, nor for the enlightenment of the people, but to create complex, intelligible, and altogether autonomous structures capable of disclosing their own immanent truth and content.

Let's digress for a moment and take a look at what all this might mean. The ability of music to disclose its inner workings, and to do so without overt reference to some "program," occurs within the context of two "species" of time: first, that of the work itself, that is, within the time it takes an interpreter to perform it, and that of historical time, to wit, time measured in years, decades, and centuries, or what the Russian philosopher Mikhail Bakhtin dubbed "great time." With repeated performances, exposure to multiple interpretations, and countless hearings, the collective expectations of listeners evolve as each new generation relates to music in new and different ways. What may influence one individual's or generation's reaction is indeterminate; any number of influential factors—social, economic, behavioral, technical, scientific, experiential, critical—come into play and affect our listening habits. Thus the impact of Beethoven's unusually rich and busy music on an early nineteenth-century audience—which, after all, was an audience accustomed to a world of horse and carriage, candlelight, and leisurely travel—would have been quite different than it is on those of us accustomed to the rush of the twenty-first century, with its plethora of electronics, air travel, and extraneous noise.

Thus, as music unfolds and gives up its secrets, we as listeners react to and are stimulated by its many ideas, but not all at once. What our ancestors heard two hundred years ago in the presence of the first performance of the Fifth Symphony (which Beethoven himself conducted) has become, for us, another kind of experience. While the opening notes of the Fifth Symphony, for example, may no longer shock us as they did those who heard them in 1808, they have lost nothing of their implicit power within the context of the work itself. In spite of the overwhelming familiarity of the motive, as something we've all known and whistled since childhood, it remains a uniquely curious and forceful element of musical rhetoric that implores us to look deeper into its relative meaning. And whatever that meaning may be, it is embedded within the very symphonic structure that informs it.

First movement: Allegro con brio (CD Track 5)

Should anyone ever ask you to define the meaning of a musical motive, you need only refer him to the opening salvo of the Fifth Symphony. Apart from the opening refrain of horns and timpani that give way to Richard Strauss's *Also Sprach Zarathustra*—a work that gained nearly equal enormous popularity after its debut as a cinematic profusion in *2001: A Space Odyssey*—it is nearly impossible to think of any figure, especially one so brief, that has become as universally recognized.

This tiny germ, which consists of only four notes, three of them repeated in rapid succession, has been tossed about for discussion with such speculative bravado over the years that one can only imagine all the things that have *not* been said about it. The most popular and widely accepted myth concerns its apparent ability to forecast the future; the now quaint statement that everyone from Beethoven himself to Napoleon is supposed to have uttered in deference to its character is "Fate knocking at the door."

If today the only thing we might hear knocking at the door is the UPS guy delivering a batch of CDs featuring yet another ten or twenty more performances of this well-worn but much-beloved masterpiece, that in no way diminishes the inherent power and substance that are responsible for its fame in the first place. Indeed, if this celebrated introductory motive suggests anything, it is ubiquity and omniscience. While it strikes us at first as nothing more than an isolated fragment given to endless repetition, its purpose and musical teleology add up to considerably more than that.

As listeners, we'd be well advised to hear the first five bars (0:01–0:11)—that is, the initial presentation followed by the repetition of the motive—as a single event. In fact, within the larger context it is part of a large melodic strand, one that continues for twenty-one bars (0:01–0:27). Thus the eighth-rests that separate its initial presentation from its second, and again from its subsequent exfoliation, form part of its immanent character. The same can be said for the two fermatas placed atop the fourth note in the first moments of the symphony (0:01–0:03; 0:07–0:11); the fermata's duty is that of prolongation, giving the performer permission to nearly double the length of the note value. But this is not so much a pause or a time for reflection so much as it is a sign of anticipation and pent-up energy. Intonatsiia, anyone?

Now let's listen to it again, this time keeping in mind this larger context. It is no accident, by the way, that Beethoven confined these first four bars to the strings, save for the inclusion of the clarinet in a largely supportive role. Though he would give the woodwinds plenty to sink their collective teeth into throughout the symphony, Beethoven eschewed any ambiguity of mood at the opening gate, as if the tessitura—that is, the higher range—and colors of the flutes, horns, and bassoons would somehow attenuate its implicit machismo.

As the motive tumbles over itself in a game of relay among the strings, intensifying in diminution, not a moment is wasted. Only a scant sixty-three bars into the movement, the anxiety is briefly dissipated by a new theme, in E-flat major, that both brightens the mood and, with only two beats per bar, slightly broadens the pace (0:59). The exposition is remarkably brief given the work's overall monumental disposition.

The ensuing development (3:17) exploits the principal motive in a playful dialogue of imitation among the strings and woodwinds. But then, unexpectedly, a consecutive string of half-notes, played *forte* astride a diminuendo, interrupt, as if to call attention to their own suspension in time (4:07). Punctuating the onset of the recapitulation (4:56), an oboe, standing in relief and all by itself, weeps slowly and quietly in diminuendo as it articulates a subtle but extended ornament (5:10). The tension mounts in an extended coda (6:32) in which a sense of urgency, brought to heel by a duple meter now grown compulsive, is brought to bear with unforgiving determination. The initial motive returns one last time, but now shared by the entire orchestra over the menacing grumble of the timpani (7:35). Seven bars of alternating dominant chords, two to a bar, flex their collective muscles as the movement draws to its defiant conclusion.

Perhaps most remarkable about this Allegro con brio is its brevity and concision. While we come away overwhelmed by its power and forthrightness, set in motion by its celebrity motive, the facts belie any musical belligerence. Listen attentively and you'll notice that the prevailing dynamic is hardly *fortissimo*, but its opposite. That's not to say that whole passages, including the opening, are not robust, and that the frequent sforzandos (which in this case Beethoven assigns more often to downbeats than to syncopations, as if to anchor the work's anxiety) are not showstoppers. But in spite of that, the development section, for the most part, purrs along like a cat ready to jump, while the no less frequent crescendos, in interpretively authoritative hands, commence, just as they should, from *piano*, en route to *forte*. Thus any notion that this movement is the love child of pomposity and swagger stands in contradiction to the compositional facts. It is essentially a quiet piece with sudden swells and violent interruptions.

These issues in turn beg the question, and nowhere with more relevance, of what role the conductor plays in interpretation and performance. Thus I digress once again as we consider and listen, on the accompanying CD, to this famous first movement. Two warring conductors of yesteryear, Hans von Bülow and Felix Weingartner, passionately disputed virtually every nuance of this and the other Beethoven symphonies, with the latter weighing in on faithful obedience to the text and the former favoring a style borne aloft more by spirit than letter. And yet both could claim victory in the debate, as there was much to be learned from their interpretive ideas and expertise, no matter its excesses born of nineteenth-century performance practices.

But it was not until decades later that certain preeminent conductors, such as Wilhelm Furtwängler and Herbert von Karajan (who both sat at the helm of the Berlin Philharmonic), likewise assumed rather different approaches to this music, which differences can, in the end, be characterized only as superficial.

Though we have no extant recordings of Bülow's conducting, by means of which we would be able to adjudicate either his reported effectiveness or allegedly wanton abandon, we have no dearth of discs with which to judge his successors. Indeed, whatever informed the aesthetic differences that distinguished Karajan from Furtwängler, each of whom recorded the Beethoven Symphonies more than once, both were in equal measure devoted to Beethoven's intentions as notated in the score. Even a cursory examination of their performances, with score in hand, reveals just how meticulous each artist was with regard to the execution of every accentuation, every note value, every dynamic gradation, and every metrical division.

If there is one striking difference, which is only generally discernible, it would be the manner in which these conductors approach a musical climax, to wit, their manipulation of rhythm as it accumulates en route to an emotional and dynamic high point. Whereas Furtwängler, like a skillful race driver on the last stretch of victory, sails into the climax with unabashed vivacity, Karajan's approach is akin to that of a tightly coiled but expertly crafted spring that, though ready to break violently at any moment, maintains its structural integrity. Another apt, if not altogether adequate metaphor, insofar as both were so religiously respectful of the score, would be to say that Furtwängler's approach favors the exogenous manipulation of dynamic tension, while Karajan prefers a more combustible interpretation, one that shrewdly stokes a composition's inner fires, like a coal that burns white-hot. Whereas Karajan, with nearly excruciating patience and aforethought, gradually brought a crescendo to a boiling point, for example, Furtwängler's overt generosity was perhaps more liquid for its overflowing exuberance.

Whatever the case, something of the myth of Furtwängler as the wildly passionate, care-to-the-winds conductor (which is not true;

he was nothing if not a stickler for detail) is in part attributable to his gawky physical appearance, with electroshock tufts of unkempt hair surrounding his bald head like a halo. As he flailed his arms and moved steedlike over the podium, he projected the air of a mad professor. The well-coiffed, silver-haired, and always elegant Karajan, on the other hand, with his Indian muftahs, was nothing if not a model for Apollonian decorum.

No one should construe these remarks as merely facetious. The physical characteristics of conductors and the way they actually appear to both the orchestra and to the audience cannot be underestimated. This dimension of performance, while admittedly not indigenous to the music itself, and thus open to accusations of irrelevance, ought not be summarily dismissed, as it does not exist in a vacuum. On the contrary, conductors' physical attributes are, or should be, substantive and capable of conveying meaning. Their vocabulary of gestures addresses the most pragmatic, albeit theatrical, aspects of a performance: the manner in which they move conveys to the musicians precisely what is wanted from them, be it the degree and rate at which a diminuendo ought secede from a *forte*, or the nature of a specific articulation (such as the aforementioned role of staccato, the function of which is to separate one pitch from another, and not an opportunity to eviscerate a tone of its breadth and resonance). Nor is their balletic athleticism a matter of indifference to listeners, either, who, as they observe conductors in action, enter into a kind of complicit musical understanding with them of what's under way. We are made privy, through a conductor's gestures, to the psychological attitude a composition projects, as well as its emotional disposition. Make no mistake: like a dancer, a conductor is also a choreographer of sorts, if not of limb, then of gesture.

What's more, masterful interpreters are as much at home in the multiple nuances of a *pianissimo* as they are in the loudest thunder stroke of a tutti. To be sure, great musicians, no matter their instrumental métier, are capable of endowing even the most serene and quiet moments of a work with near vibratory intensity, that is, with a certain fullness of tone and temperament that more than one romantic critic has described as "a steel hand in a velvet glove."

Second movement: Andante con moto

It's no wonder that Beethoven labored for years over the initial theme of this stirring Andante, altering its pitch material, rhythm, and trajectory until he got it just right. And when he did, it took no fewer than twenty-two bars to establish in its entirety, perhaps a record for a theme of this sort. It is not so much a tune that in turn is developed or fragmented, as it is a lyrical effusion that proceeds at its own pace and is made subject to thoughtful commentary, like a series of afterthoughts, en route to its first cadence.

The melodic line is fluid; the principal tune, taking up three beats per bar, sallies forth in a gracious train of dotted notes played by the violins and cellos, to a supportive but uneventful accompaniment in the basses. The mood is optimistic in the relative major key of E-flat, for which Beethoven, throughout his life, seemed to hold a special affection. The woodwinds move in only eight bars later, yielding a variant of the initial motive, but one that strikes us resigned, even conciliatory. The strings, patient and in the wings, reenter and give echo to the woodwinds' lackadaisical song.

Already Beethoven is setting things up formally as a set of variations on a theme. But as he is no ordinary musical architect, he has resolved to mix form with fantasy. Just as an architect might look for the most effective way to organize space and to take advantage of the play of light both on and into a structure, so does Beethoven find opportunities to introduce the unexpected into otherwise perfectly conventional territory. Thus in the second phase of the opening, a new theme, at once proud and vaguely military in its disposition, discreetly and quietly lunges forward. A few bars later, the entire orchestra bellows in *fortissimo*, with this new theme, now fully robust, entrusted to the woodwinds above a stream of relentless and widely spaced triplets carried by the strings below. The timpani, too, lend gravity and a certain pugnaciousness. But things quiet down soon enough on the way to the next cadence, which is reached with a certain tenuousness just as the first variation makes its move. The melody, now shorn of its dots, that is, of its short-to-long values, is rendered in musical plain-speak.

Yet another variation ensues, this time in a river of easygoing thirty-second-notes, culminating in a bass-laden restatement of the theme's remaining content. Yet with each successive appearance of the aforementioned second (or thirty-second-note "pride") theme, which finds its way back soon enough, the mood grows more confident and entitled. Now the woodwinds, supported by trumpets and timpani, speak out without fear, their voices loud and ringing. Again, as if in contemplation of what had just transpired, the flutes and clarinets grab on to a mere fragment of the initial theme and toss it about in a minor modality with blithe disregard for the dutiful arpeggiation given to the accompanying strings.

When the principal theme establishes itself, it is fleshed out *fortissimo* by the entire ensemble and is no longer so pliant or sweet. On the contrary, it has in this, its final statement, become gigantic, solid, granitic, and impenetrable. Sauntering almost unnoticed within these musical walls is a canon, that is, melodic imitation, divvied up among the strings and woodwinds. What a pity that the dynamic properties of the passage, now in a double *forte*, overwhelm this playful innovation. Perhaps that is something for certain conductors, who ignore its potential, to think about! A short but spirited coda attempts to accelerate things by means of dotted figures juxtaposed with rapid triplets, but these are almost immediately cut down to size and dismissed for their impatience, perhaps in a symbolic swipe at the inefficacy of weakness. A rumble of triplets wells up suddenly, like a distant storm, in the bass and inspires the woodwinds to take up rhythmic arms with it. The last few measures give voice to the triumph of the tonic and render definitive what had been a most varied, if progressive, rumination.

Third movement: Allegro; Trio

Beethoven certainly had a way with arpeggios. That he could turn the most mundane and innocuous compositional element into an occasion for philosophical regard is just as astonishing in this scherzo-like Allegro as it is at the opening of the "Eroica" Symphony. Here C minor make its understated return, enshrouded in mystery; the first three bars, given over entirely to the cellos and basses, outline a simple C minor triad that seems to emerge from offstage, as it were, in a whispery *pianissimo*. They stand alone until joined, ever so quietly and cautiously, by the violins and the woodwinds a few moments later.

But this entire introductory passage, though hardly inconsequential, serves only to foreshadow the main theme of the A section, which by now sounds awfully familiar. And it should: it is none other than a variant of the four-note motive that opens the first movement. But here the horns announce, with unapologetic determination, the figure's arrival. It doesn't take long before the horns, like political protagonists at a protest rally, persuade the rest of the orchestra to likewise proclaim the same. But the mood now is more strident than somber, as it was in the first movement; having already earned its place, the motive, even in its slightly altered state (all four notes are identical here; there is no descent, as in the first movement, to the third below), is perhaps more declarative than ambitious.

Never veering too far off the path of conventional classical decorum, Beethoven, as expected, airs these fragments again, lending them more power and instrumental forces the second time out, until the violins trouble themselves with a new motive. This new arrival is a quiet though nervous patch of eighth-notes interspersed with a quarter-note at the end of each of the three bars in which they have been placed, then tied up, at the end of the phrase, with three assertive quarter-notes that land squarely on the strong beats.

Don't worry; even with all this talk of note values, you hardly need a score to recognize this figure, which is not only distinct from the earlier motives, but immediately precedes the gruff fugato of the ensuing trio. Here C minor becomes C major, converting itself to the new tonal territory with all the fervor of a religious zealot, giving a whole new meaning to the term C section. The audacious onslaught of eighth-notes that inform it is a departure from the usual character of the form; there are no yelping horn calls here, or even the remotest suggestion, actual or metaphorical, of a provincial fox hunt. Instead, the string section attacks its new figure with unrepentant guts and verve, relying on long and vigorous bows to convey a most unstudious *pesante*.

The return of the A section, again in C minor, is unusual for its skimpiness. Beethoven has narrowed the texture considerably, making bare bones of what had been the rather rich if silky sheen of its first incarnation. The clarinets and oboes bleat the four-note motive with timorous uncertainty, accompanied by the strings, which on this occasion trace the arpeggio figure in a pinched pizzicato (unlike staccato, the note values modified by pizzicato—the plucking of the strings—truly are short and not merely separated). Elsewhere, a continuous pedal point (that is, the repetition of a single pitch in duration) asserts itself in the timpani in *pianissimo*. After some forty-three bars of this, the orchestra regains its mass in a virulent crescendo that swells rapidly and segues without pause into the heroic Finale.

Fourth movement: Allegro

The influence of this finale to end all finales on so much of the later music of the nineteenth century cannot be underestimated. It shares a camaraderie of spirit and intent, if you will, with innumerable works, both great and not so great, whose composers were as inspired as they were overwhelmed. For example, more than twenty-five years later, Robert Schumann saw fit to dub the last movement of his famous piano suite *Carnaval*, Op. 9, "March of the Davidsbündler against the Philistines." While both the title and the fearless bravado of the march itself bears within it all kinds of literary allusions in its perhaps anachronistic nod to the French Revolution (or more accurately, toward what the French Revolution stood for: liberty, fraternity, spiritual enlightenment), there can be no doubt that the Fifth Symphony, and especially this allegro, were its inspiration.

The emotional climate here, born of optimism, forthrightness, and stubborn fortitude, is so obvious (so much so that a few contemporary critics found it to be cheap and vulgar, and nothing more or less than a reservoir of effects, rather than affects) as to dismiss as unnecessary any structural or harmonic analysis. Of course, while there is a certain wisdom that befits the naiveté of that position, abandoning analysis in favor of instinct alone would serve only to blindside the more substantive dimensions that inform the work and render its bluster as something more significant and profound. Even so, here is yet another instance of Freud's famous cigar; sometimes things just are not what they seem to be.

Marches, or marchlike works (as this is, strictly speaking), are earmarked for stridency, if not by virtue of their rhythmic construction, then for their purpose. Lurking behind nearly every march, no matter how innocuous, is the specter of a military banner, a collective voice of patriotic pride, and a certain xenophobic centralism. While no one can or ought to accuse Beethoven of lowering his compositional standards to accommodate merely programmatic fervor, he leaves us with the unmistakable impression that something along the lines of resistance and the aforementioned notion of overcoming (adversity) dwells at its core. After all, this movement puts to work every instrument of the orchestra, often at the same time, as it fulfills its potential: the huge sonorities, the legion of bellowing *fortissimos*, the endlessly propulsive rhythms articulated in rapid succession, the unfettered appropriation of downbeats to drive home a harmonic point, and not least, the sovereign authority of its overall timbre and trajectory all contribute to an atmosphere of might and determination. Victory is its not-so-hidden agenda, even if that victory is one of form over content, or content over form.

In its formal construction, it offers nothing out of the ordinary, though Beethoven rejects a return to C minor in favor of the far sunnier and more hopeful tonality of C major. Themes are presented and developed, cadences are carefully positioned, and various ideas, which had already germinated throughout the entire symphony, are revisited. The initial theme, awash in bravado and carried forward loudly by the entire orchestra, is as straightforward a melodic postulate as it is fresh and invigorating. The woodwinds, horns, and especially a triumvirate of trombones predominate, lending both weight and character to the proceedings.

The overall ascent of the pitch patterns in consecutive eighth notes is not merely a consequence of their temporal organization, but an investment in melodic destiny; in other words, as the melody is borne aloft in an upward trajectory, it articulates its own dénouement and, by proxy, the notion of fate itself. In response to this profusion, emboldened still more by regularly recurring if sometimes disruptive sforzandos attached to both strong and weak beats, there emerges, like a wizened general riding into battle, a rather derivative second theme, again proffered by the horns and woodwinds.

Soon enough, after the feverish traversal of a third melodic fragment, we run headlong into a fourth figure of ascending triplets in the dominant key, G major. These triplets strike me as a reaction to the stern and by now nearly antediluvian pronouncement of the symphony's opening four-note motive. Indeed, as these dart forward energetically in swift succession toward an accentuated quarter-note, they become something of an anti-motive, in that they seek to liberate themselves from the dour seriousness of the symphony's opening salvo. The development section exploits their potential without delay, first by giving leave to the basses to reverse, almost imperceptibly, their direction, and then by cross-pollinating the figure in imitation among all the instruments.

A remarkable and certainly brave bit of musical panache surfaces on the horizon of the recapitulation. Without warning, a slight slackening of tempo plays midwife to a familiar theme, namely, the initial four-note motive of the preceding movement (Allegro), as if it had been wandering about the whole time but had taken a wrong turn. In the hands of an inferior composer, its inclusion would have been merely banal, but in this context it is a sobering reminder of a distant and perhaps less optimistic world.

The recapitulation bulldogs its way into our consciousness as it recycles all the forgoing thematic material. Conventional means of rhythmic intensification, not the least of which are underlying trills in the strings, complement the litany of familiar tunes as shrill waves of piccolos burst forth from on high. Suddenly, the pace picks up; yet another motivic variant of the four-note motive, this time distinguished by its speed (presto) and compulsiveness, pummels the compositional landscape with ruthless determination. The Fifth Symphony concludes its business in a brazen chordal fanfare.

An afterthought inspired by the Fifth Symphony

Now we come to another issue, which this symphony raises in particular. It is a thorny subject for professional musicians that has likewise lingered tenuously in the minds of amateur listeners for some time. While this subject will form the basis for a lengthier discussion in my forthcoming book for Amadeus Press on the piano music of Franz Liszt, it also has relevance here. What I refer to, of course, is the role and, indeed, the entire phenomenon of the *transcription*.

By the mid-nineteenth century, the transcription, which the *New Harvard Dictionary of Music* aptly describes as "the adaptation of a composition for a medium other than its original one," had become all the rage. Though as a genre in its own right it was certainly nothing new, having grown out of a tradition that reached back as far as the fourteenth century, it assumed new and practical importance by the early 1800s. Composers were often asked by their publishers or pressured by an adoring public to transcribe their instrumental works, especially orchestral and chamber music, for piano. This practice allowed the average consumer, living in rural or less populated areas with no or limited access to concert life in major urban centers, to become familiar with themes that were seemingly on everyone's lips. In an era when neither recordings nor high-speed transportation even existed, transcriptions made it possible to belt out on a keyboard the endearing tunes and inspiring rhythms of a Beethoven or Mozart, no matter how compromised those often neglected, out-of-tune rural instruments might have been.

While this was most certainly a productive development that made it possible for the general population to cultivate at least some knowledge of—and more important, a love for—great music, it also had a downside. Many composers penned transcriptions as yet one more means to make money. Others, like Beethoven, disdained the practice, at least when his own music, transcribed by anyone other than himself, was concerned. He admitted his distaste for the genre, even though he himself penned a transcription of one of his early piano sonatas for a string quartet, as well as his Second Symphony for a piano trio. "The *unnatural mania* at present day," he wrote to his publisher, Breitkopf and Härtel, "to wish to transfer *pieces for the piano forte* to string instruments which in every way are so different, ought to be stopped!"

So why, given the widespread acceptance and even the usefulness of transcriptions, is a conductor or an orchestra even necessary? Why can't a great symphony, such as Beethoven's Fifth, be performed by a competent pianist or a skilled chamber ensemble? What difference would it make, and wouldn't the music, in its new clothing, so to speak, exert the same effect on its listener as the original? After all, music is music, and the pitch and rhythm material is identical in both versions, even if the instruments are not.

Well, the answer is simple. Things are not at all the same. The net effect of a piano transcription on our way of listening, that is, the manner in which we relate to the music itself, is an entirely different experience. The affective stimulation that only an orchestra can provide, on the other hand, fuels our emotional response to musical experience; a piano reduction—and make no mistake, that is precisely what it is: a reduction—remains wholly unsatisfactory in comparison.

Indeed, in preparing this book, I referred to Beethoven's orchestral scores as well as Liszt's piano transcriptions. While a useful tool for study, the piano versions, even from Liszt's ingenious mind, pale next to the real thing. Unlike his paraphrases of French and German operas, wherein he elaborates the principal themes of an aria or overture, turning them into wholly autonomous piano works, Liszt's arrangements of the Beethoven Symphonies are nothing if not faithful to the originals. Nowhere does he degrade either their letter or spirit. On the contrary, he approaches the task of symphonic transcription with consummate decorum and dignity, refusing to indulge in pianistic effects for their own sake. His agenda was clear: to convey the substance of Beethoven's musical ideas, which he did admirably.

And yet, ironically, that is precisely why they fall short; these symphonies were not, nor were they ever intended to be, piano music. These worthy and certainly useful transcriptions cannot in any way convey either the immanent character of the instrumentation or the complexity of the orchestration. To be sure, as we begin to study these works in earnest, we realize these elements are not merely material properties, but artistic ones, just as carefully adjudicated by the composer (and interpreter) as the notes and rhythms he sets to paper. They are in fact indigenous to the music itself.

In playing the transcriptions on the piano, we miss the ardency of the strings as they swell or diminish; we long for the plaintive reediness of a single lonely oboe, the breathy vivacity of a flute, and the menacing vibrations of the timpani. The shimmer of a vibrato or the airy aspiration of a distant horn call cannot be effectively duplicated (though they might be suggested) with octave tremolos and pedaling tricks. Thus, in the absence of the spirited interplay of parts and instrumental colors, far too much gets lost in the translation. While it is an ambitious and tempting challenge for a pianist to live up to all that, it is quite impossible, as it is largely by virtue of the instrumentarium, made whole by the music that something far more powerful and intimate stands to be realized by an orchestra.

Even in the few recordings pianists have made of these works, the divide between the ambiance of the orchestral and its keyboard counterpart becomes significant, sometimes embarrassingly so. Even Glenn Gould, who often carried off performances of piano transcriptions with unusual aplomb, could not rescue Liszt's transcription of the Fifth Symphony, in his otherwise fascinating recording, from its essential banality. That much is obvious. A piano is a piano, after all, and no matter how imaginative the pianist or how luxurious the instrument, in the end, it is not a collection of violins and cellos, oboes, clarinets, trumpets, and timpani, but a large box wired with strings, the sound of which diminishes almost immediately upon striking them. What's more, the tone quality of a string or woodwind instrument, while something a particularly savvy pianist may be able to imaginatively convey if not duplicate, is unique. Each is imbued with its own special color and, when combined with other instruments, attains to a synthetic timbre the quality of which is incomparable.

Of course, it is unlikely that anyone would be so naïve or completely daft as to simply dismiss the role of instrumentation in the symphonies of Beethoven (or any other composer for that matter) as either interchangeable or, worse, musically insignificant. At the same time, to extol transcriptions, especially those arranged for piano, as being adequate to the task of conveying the musical substance of their original counterparts strikes me as ludicrous. Certainly, anyone who cares to take a deeper look into the compositional structure and organization of these magnificent works will find the transcriptions of Liszt to be an exceptionally useful source, especially when used alongside the orchestral scores.

Symphony No. 6 in F Major, Op. 68 ("Pastoral")

Piccolo, 2 Flutes, 2 Oboes, 2 Clarinets (B-flat), 2 Bassoons, 2 Horns (F, B-flat), 2 Trumpets (C, E-flat), Alto Trombone, Tenor Trombone, Timpani, Violins I and II, Violas, Cellos, Basses

Completed in 1808

First performance: Theater-an-der-Wien, Vienna, December 22, 1808

Dedicated to Prince von Lobkowitz and Count Razumovsky

First movement: Awakening of serene impressions on arriving in the country—Allegro ma non troppo
Second movement: Scene by the brookside—Andante molto moto
Third movement: Jolly gathering of country folk—Allegro
Fourth movement: Thunderstorm. Tempest—Allegro
Fifth movement: Shepherd's Song. Gladsome and thankful feelings after the storm—Allegretto

In the vast hierarchy of symphonic literature from Mozart to the present day, the "Pastoral" Symphony occupies a unique place. What sets it apart is not something attributable to the fame of its composer, nor to its overtly programmatic content, but the broader role it played in the aesthetics of its day.

While it would be a gross exaggeration to say that the "Pastoral" Symphony was in some significant way a direct consequence of the burgeoning fascination in the symbolic potential of landscape painting and poetry in the early nineteenth century, it would not be going too far afield to surmise, at the very least, that it paved the way for the tremendous influence of those art forms on music. By the end of the eighteenth century, the métier of the landscape had taken on new meaning. No longer was bucolic imagery, either in French or English landscape painting, tied to any historical or religious event, but came into its own as a symbol of evolution, which is to say, progress.

Indeed, in conformity with the aesthetics of their day, painters and poets, like their counterparts in music, imbued their landscape paintings, poems, and descriptive prose with a certain autonomy. The landscape was no longer merely a backdrop against which people or property were portrayed, but a living, breathing emblem of the forces, and thus the spirit of change. The landscape, with its fauna, wildlife, play of light, and geological artifacts, was itself an opportunity to contemplate the passage of time and the essence of evolution. By the early nineteenth century, the landscape had become an artistic opportunity that required, if it were to convey the artist's or the author's ideas, considerable specificity—of place, time, and character. What's more, the landscape came to be viewed as a metaphor for history itself; great poets, such as Wordsworth, Coleridge, and Goethe, along with such celebrated painters as Friedrich, Corot, and Constable, made of this deepening descriptive genre something on the order of a musical experience.

But in spite of the random and apparent disorder of the natural environment in what existentialism would later celebrate as the exigencies of a chaotic universe, these artists discerned something no less profound. In the image of a rock there was the theme of strength and endurance; in a flower the theme of growth, dissolution, and death; in mist and fog the theme of memory and regret; and in sunlight (and moonlight) the theme of season, eternity, and hope.

In the "Pastoral" Symphony, Beethoven offers a view of nature that is perhaps not as specifically contemplative as it is a musical overview. Again, as he had in his earlier symphonies, he appropriates conventional compositional strategies and forms and reinvents them. Thus many of the compositional devices used by his predecessors—horn calls to represent a hunt or simply a distant memory; an oboe or flute to evoke birdsong; and timpani and strings, in a flurry of tremolos, to suggest a storm—are here presented without any sentimentality or pointless bravado. It is as if Beethoven has shorn these nature images, not quite cultivated to the degree of ideational specificity that poets and painters would later bring to them, of anything but their fundamental suggestiveness.

Even so, as the entire symphony is given over to this concept, and in such grand scale, it can only have inspired his contemporaries in the plastic and literary arts.

First movement: Awakening of serene impressions on arriving in the country—Allegro ma non troppo

In spite of its overall quiescence, to say that the first movement of the "Pastoral" is uneventful would be to deny its compositional integrity. Its simplicity is deceptive, given the overall sophistication of its structural underpinnings. Indeed, the entire movement proceeds from only two fundamental themes, if you can call them that; both are tightly knit motivic fragments of four bars each, which expand and contract dynamically and in moderation. In duple meter, the mood set forth is gracious and unhurried, as if it didn't have a care in the world. There are no extended crescendos or diminuendos to be found here, nor any of the abrupt sforzandos of the sort we have grown accustomed to in Beethoven's other symphonies. Nor do we encounter the embattled dissonances that throughout much of his other music render ideas of conflict and antagonism so palpably and effectively. On the contrary, in this Allegro, all is calm. Even where the Beethoven pits the first theme against triplets, as he does throughout the development, there is no hint of unsteadiness or conflict, rhythmic or otherwise.

If, in this cheerful collective of motivic fragments, Beethoven's objective was to create the impression of the countryside, he succeeds precisely because of the restraint he imposes on both form and content. The first theme, for example, is nothing more than a tidy but deftly articulated group of eighth notes in close spatial proximity, punctuated by two sixteenths. It is a playful and uneventful anapest, at first taken on by the violins before being passed over to the oboe and then the flutes. Certainly, it is the consistent, even unabashed, repetition of this motive that renders it somewhat innocuous; it makes no grand statement. Its purpose is hardly to ruffle feathers, but to portray them. The second theme, too, a fluid, gently descending stream of eighth-notes, sports an air at once friendly and inviting.

Of course, the title of the movement leaves it up to the imagination of the listener to discern what any particular theme may refer to: a brook, the rustle of leaves, a ray of sunlight, a gentle breeze that moves along a wistful cloud overhead, or the distant reveries of the towns-folk. Of all the words in that title, however, none is more suggestive than "Awakenings," for that is exactly what appears to be going on in this work, even when abstracted from metaphor: a kind of musical awakening exemplified by whole sequences of motivic exchanges. This fruit of this is nowhere more apparent than in the development, where the anapestic first motive is tossed about with ease and casual abandon among the strings and woodwinds, only occasionally bloating itself in periodic unisons in all the instruments. Every modulation appears to augur something fresh and unheard, though always within the identical motivic and rhythmic context of the two ever-so-familiar thematic fragments.

Again, the sense of time engendered by this movement is neither oppressive nor eventful, but progressive. That in itself is an invisible metaphor for natural evolution. Neither of the principal motives is subjected to much variance, and what alterations they do undergo are subtle and gradual, just as if Nature herself had been responsible for their immanent cultivation.

But if I may indulge a personal observation, the usefulness of which is no less subjective or theoretically relevant than anyone's experience of this music, it is this: as I write this analysis and listen to the "Pastoral," I am taking in a magnificent view to the east from the upper story of my farmhouse in rural Vermont. It is late afternoon, the light has begun to dim, and it is snowing steadily. Overhead, the sky envelops the scene in an even gray. A new blanket has already covered the intricately woven branches of the patch of apple trees just outside the house. The rest of the land is clear, its panorama so wide that I can actually discern, as if in miniature, the curvature of the earth. The land, sloping gently to the east, is articulated by a row of firs and leafless maples that, at

a distance of about a quarter mile to the east and also to the north,
define the landscape, but that have likewise faded into the flaky deluge.
The wizened, jagged peak of Mount Monadnock in neighboring New
Hampshire, which is normally visible from my window, has disappeared
completely beneath the snow and sky. Indeed, these have now hemor-
rhaged almost imperceptibly one into the other, as if they were attached
by a thread, obscuring all but the outlines of the thickest branches in a
foggy apparition of light and shadow.

While these images hardly bring to mind the springtime ambiance
that the first movement of the "Pastoral" so often does for so many, I
cannot help thinking that the associative imagery is really no less potent
or subliminal than in any other nature scene. In combination with the
gentility of the music, and its no less affective motivic brushstrokes,
the harmonic patina of the landscape is somehow amplified by the
presence of the music, which seems to inform its symmetry or even its
lack thereof.

These bucolic images, for all their loveliness, reveal nothing of the
compositional realities of the "Pastoral" Symphony, nor even bear any
actual relationship to it. The theorists, ready to thrash me for even
daring to suggest it, are on this point correct. And yet it is easy to
understand something else, at least from where I am sitting, and that
is just how powerful a hold the "Pastoral" Symphony's lucid rhythms
and docile harmonies must have had on its audiences of 1808. Like all
music, it inspires reverie and a litany of associative images, which are
different for each individual. Yet to dismiss the Allegro's cozy, placid
ambiance as merely ineffectual or irrelevant strikes me as a rather
crude attempt to undermine the *esthesic* (a term not to be mistaken for
aesthetic) potential of musical experience, to wit, the manner in which
we respond to musical stimuli in the context of a socialized environment. It is perhaps, too, no little irony that it was a theorist and musical
semiologist, Jean-Jacques Nattiez, who coined that term and who, in
so doing, opened up the interpretation of music to something greater
than the sum of its material parts.

In tracing the rhythmic anapest (two short values followed by a long
one) that fleshes out virtually every bar of this introductory movement,
even bringing it to a close with the chirping of a lone flute, we are

struck by how subtle, yet powerful, is its cumulative value. Decades later, Robert Schumann would pay tribute to the identical figure, and perhaps to the "Pastoral" itself, in his energetic and anything but pastoral *Humoresque* for piano, Op. 20, likewise adjudicating, for a full half hour, the energetic potential of this small fragment.

Second movement: Scene by the brookside—Andante molto moto

The ambulatory, even Italianate, elegance of this Andante, composed in 12/8 time, would later inspire the water imagery of much other music of the romantic era, not the least of which, one might think, is Chopin's *Barcarolle*. In the dominant key of B-flat major, the first violins waste no time in introducing their melodic charge, a lilting but delicately embroidered melody set to a dulcet accompaniment in descending thirds, likewise played by the strings. As the second violins evolve into a group of continuous sixteenths, we are once again put in mind of the much-maligned role of "accompaniment." Here the notes do more than merely languish as a means of filling in the prevailing harmony. Rather, their purpose is to at once enrich the texture as they provide an underlying stream (an intentional metaphor if ever there was one) upon which the principal melody is carried along.

As the principal melody is further elaborated and passed liberally among the clarinets, flutes, and strings, the horns purr gently and quietly in the background, venturing their support in open fifths and octaves throughout. The horns seed the music here, investing in it something of the aura of an offstage overlooking the action. Even where the principal material migrates, first into G major and then E-flat, the aquatic sixteenths continue to drone on beneath the surface, carrying the theme along with it in an irresistible musical current.

Suddenly, as the end draws near, Beethoven, meticulous as always, offers an entirely unambiguous nod to the work's programmatic content in an evocation of the songs of three birds: a nightingale, a quail, and a cuckoo, played by a solo flute, oboe, and clarinet, respectively. Rather than leave the identity of these birdcalls to the imagination of the listener or even posterity, Beethoven explicitly refers to them as such in the score. So much for an analysis that would merely reject as pointless the role of extramusical reference in this or any other work of Beethoven.

Third movement: Jolly gathering of country folk— Allegro

While it is sorely tempting to invent any number of fanciful scenarios for this movement, a scherzo in tone and character, it speaks well enough for itself. While Berlioz and others have intuited in this movement the reveries of mountain folk—all outfitted, no doubt, in lederhosen and agog at the quality of the wine harvest—something far more remarkable is afoot: the ingenuity of the work itself.

Things begin blithely enough as the violins and violas, joined a few bars later by their cousins the basses and cellos, sketch a relatively uneventful thematic murmur. The melody's descent from a high F to an A more than an octave below gives way to a wholly new theme in D major, also eight bars in length but this time enriched by the flutes. As if impatient with their own proclivities, these themes, now in tandem, grow restless in a kind of urgent consolidation of the material at hand. As the horns burst forth in octaves and interrogative sforzandos, the mood has brightened and the dynamic becomes *fortissimo;* the addition of a trumpet illuminates the orchestral texture that much more. In this merry mélange the horns again attain prominence, sporting their by now well-known hunting call in thirds and open fifths.

If indeed the chase is on, then where are the foxes? Rather than introducing myriad new elements in an attempt to musically depict activities that surround such an occasion—the bustle of people, the neighing and gallops of the steeds, the barking of the hounds, and so on—Beethoven does just the opposite. Only moments later, a single oboe, accompanied by the violins in a seemingly offstage echo of the aforementioned horn call, inaugurates the trio. The theme here, at once unaffected and carefree, exemplifies bucolic calm, suggesting the plainsong of an itinerant Alpine shepherd who, leading his herd of bleating unshorn sheep, pipes his way toward yet another imaginary landscape.

While that is indeed a pleasant tableau to contemplate, there is something more substantial to consider in the household of compositional procedure. For one thing, this folksy thematic confection bears a slight resemblance to the second theme of the movement's opening, in that its quarter-note contours likewise angle upward in intervals of a third, only to be briefly punctuated by two eighth-notes. In close pursuit, a clarinet and a horn then take charge of this motivic material. But then, without warning, the meter hastens in stretto, leading us again to experience the compression of time. Indeed, the prevailing triple meter, the *sine qua non* of a scherzo, inexplicably becomes duple, converting itself into a rustic peasant dance. Here, the violins, supported by the sforzando foot stomping of the cellos and basses, tumble forward with an earthy, even crude four-bar motive as the flutes chirp frivolously in triplets above. The customary and usual repeat of the first section ensues, followed by an abbreviated coda that segues forcefully into the next movement, one of the most famous in the history of the symphonic literature.

Fourth movement: Thunderstorm; Tempest—Allegro
(CD Track 6)

There are those who view this tour de force of descriptive music as little more than an effective transition from the Scherzo to the Finale, but not as a movement in its own right. While there is certainly merit to an argument that characterizes its deliberate bluster as merely incidental, it is also an interpretation that would seek to diminish both its function and its autonomy within a larger context.

Had Beethoven considered this bit of the "Pastoral" so insignificant, it is hardly likely he would have bothered investing it with a moniker all its own, just as he did with its sister movements. And though it may be tied by a musical umbilical cord to the preceding Scherzo and to the ensuing Finale, its independence in both formal and structural categories is assured; it belongs to neither the former nor the latter.

A tenuous tremolo in the cellos and basses introduces the work (0:00), followed almost immediately by the second violins, which usher in a stream of evenly articulated eighths in contrasting directions (0:04). The first violins add their two cents moments later with an ominous three-note fragment characterized by a diminished fifth (0:07). The timpani, which make their one and only appearance in this symphony in this movement, and for a very specific purpose, annihilate the prevailing *pianissimo* with the first clap of musical thunder (0:31) in the form of a blistering, *fortissimo* trill.

Riding astride this unsettling but palpable vibration is a train of sixteen sixteenth-notes per bar in the bass pitted against a contrasting rhythm of twenty such notes in the cellos; the later instruments play five notes per beat against four notes played by the former. Though nearly imperceptible in such a low register, the rhythmic conflict set up by this five-against-four rhythm is nonetheless disturbing and conveys its inner antagonism with conviction. Adding to the intensity is a sequence of descending arpeggios and diminished chords (0:34). Then, like Jupiter hurling thunderbolts, a confident, aggressive new figure in vigorously adjudicated eighth-notes, and commencing from an unforgiving sforzando, takes center stage (0:51), but not for long. The murky underpinnings of the bass, still enamored of its run of sixteenths (0:59), are violently interrupted by a sequence of rough-and-tumble rhythmic fragments, played by the strings and winds as they grab hold of yet more sforzandos, as if for dear life (1:12).

The eighth-note figure of the opening now returns (1:17), again in the violins, but now with renewed purpose and no little anxiety. A skillfully entwined crescendo thrusts the entire orchestra forward into a brazen conflagration of all the instruments, including two trombones and piccolo (1:48). Given the energetic burst born of the instrumentation and sequences of unresolved harmonies, it is as if the eye of the storm, be it musical or meteorological, is nowhere to be seen. Instead, the fury of this artistic storm is betrayed by a compositional pounding of sorts, wherein motivic material, so strictly yet economically dispatched in symmetrical periods, is buffeted mercilessly by the tonal winds. The emboldened second theme, which as you will recall is made up of pugnacious eighth-notes, makes another appearance (2:05), only to be itself rebuffed by a descending chromatic scale (2:13). The shrill strain of a piccolo on high exacerbates an already anxious situation, while the timpani yet again tremble in thunderous trills (2:27).

But by now the worst is over, at least in metaphorical categories. A long diminuendo, led by the strings (2:45), signals the end of the furies, as the storm, whatever its aesthetic etiology, dissipates and moves into the distance. Here an oboe emerges, as surely as the sun emerges from behind a once ominous cloud, with a brief but hopeful refrain (3:41). Finally, a lone flute, at once relieved at the passing of the turbulence and inspired by the hopeful song of the oboe, asserts itself with its own meek summation as it segues to the song of gratitude, which is the Finale (4:01).

Fifth movement: Shepherd's Song; Gladsome and thankful feelings after the storm—Allegretto

One would have to be entirely immune to Beethoven's symbolic language in failing to appreciate the role of the clarinet and horns that open this concluding Allegretto. The initial theme, given over to the horns and clarinets, expresses itself in distended intervals of fourths and sixths as it hovers gently over open fifths in the violas, cellos, and basses. Its musical etiology is apparent: here we get wind of yet another bucolic horn call, this time given voice in the unruffled, even circular metrical ambiance of six beats to the bar. The violins take up the rustic melody within minutes, only to flirt again with the woodwinds, which decline to abandon it.

Even so, the tune gains confidence, swelling from a quiescent *pianissimo* to a rousing *fortissimo* with the horns, violas, and cellos in unison. But then, as if not to be outwitted, the violins introduce a new if somewhat more urgent theme that takes up only two bars. Its optimistic upward trajectory, elaborated in trills and then in sequences of descending eighths and sixteenths, eventually yields to a return of the original theme. Only measures later, the clarinets and bassoons jump in with a no less lilting though unusually expansive theme that stretches through twelve bars. But the principal theme is never far behind, surfacing continually throughout the movement, just as it should in this, a fairly traditional rondo form.

While the reiterations of the few themes that constitute this movement give us pause to contemplate Beethoven's ingenuity, it would be a disservice to the programmatic intentions of this movement, no less than the others, to ignore its extramusical proclivities. Certainly, no one can blame Berlioz, who opined with romantic ardor second to none that in this movement "the sky is serene; the rain is almost gone, and the shepherds reappear upon the mountains, calling together their scattered flocks." But such opulent, metaphor-rich imagery, while colorful, is perhaps not as revealing as a simpler, albeit conceptual abstraction. Indeed, from the opening bars, which in their reverie suggest calm after the storm, this Allegretto is nothing if not an exceptionally personal statement. Its simplicity of form, which sustains and supports its content in a relatively slow harmonic rhythm (that is, the pace at which the prevailing harmony at any given moment changes), is in itself an abstract expression of faith and goodwill, its character at once beneficent and prayerful.

Symphony No. 7
in A Major, Op. 92

2 Flutes, 2 Oboes, 2 Clarinets, 2 Bassoons,
2 Horns, 2 Trumpets (D), Timpani, Violins I and II,
Violas, Cellos, Basses

Completed in the summer of 1812

First performance, conducted by the composer,
on December 8, 1813, University of Vienna

Dedicated to Count Moritz von Fries

First movement: Poco sostenuto; Vivace
Second movement: Allegretto
Third movement: Presto; Assai meno presto;
   Tempo primo
Fourth movement: Allegro con brio

Now a middle-aged man-about-town who just happened to be as much of a celebrity as he was a cause célèbre, Beethoven could certainly speak of 1811 and 1812 as being among his banner years. He composed both the Seventh and Eighth Symphonies in 1812, which was a tremendous achievement in its own right. In the same year, Jane Austen's luscious romance about failed relationships and the emotional poverty of materialism proved an indictment of the burgeoning optimism of the day, while elsewhere, devastating earthquakes left Caracas in ruins and rerouted the Mississippi River. Insanity took on new meaning when the doddering King George of England was declared insane and his throne was taken over by his namesake, George, Prince of Wales.

The cultural climate, as the century entered its second decade, entered a murkier phase; Europe, all agog over its spiritual liberation, suddenly began to experience something along the lines of self-doubt. After much soul-searching in the wake of its long fascination with aesthetic contemplation, the intelligentsia, now en route to romanticism, was again reexamining its own values. Perhaps it is no coincidence that both Chopin and Liszt were born, in 1810 and 1811, respectively, into this tenuous environment.

Something of the Seventh Symphony's gargantuan dimensions reflect this changing sensibility. Like the virulent seismic waves that rocked two continents thousands of miles away as he penned this symphony, Beethoven unleashed musical forces that both invigorated and perplexed his listeners. Indeed, the sight of the entirely deaf Beethoven conducting the Seventh at its premiere in Vienna was doubtless inspiring in its own right.

First movement: Poco sostenuto; Vivace

This Seventh Symphony is nothing if not an exercise in the cumulative power of rhythm. The stately sostenuto introduction is simple enough in both design and structure. Following a brief statement in half-notes played first by the oboes and then by the clarinets, the mood intensifies in an upward parade of sixteenths in the strings. The oboes gently articulate a second subject, its intervals closely positioned, before being echoed by the violins.

After a detour through a series of E-naturals played by the winds and strings, the entrance of a lively Vivace is distinguished by a rhythmic ostinato in 6/8 time. This theme, characterized by a breathy dotted rhythm, is given over first to the flutes but then to the first violins. The second violins and violas offer an assertive accompaniment while the trumpets and timpani, stubbornly alighting on a single pitch, refuse to let go of the dotted rhythm. Nothing that could properly be referred to as a second theme ever emerges, as if to say that the expressive power of a single idea was quite enough.

The development section combines the motivic capital of the introductory sostenuto—the rising scales—with the dotted figure that assures the vivace its stature. In short order, each instrumental group is engulfed by a series of poco crescendos that reach their fever in *fortissimo* and in anticipation of the return of the first theme. A fragment of the dotted theme is strewn liberally among the winds and strings in a playful dialogue, only to be usurped by the return of the principal theme in the violins. The movement's conclusion is rendered all the more inevitable by the none-too-precarious resurgence of the dotted motive in the tutti ably supported by brightly blaring trumpets and the no-less-insistent timpani.

Second movement: Allegretto (CD Track 7)

Although the leisurely tempo indicated by Allegretto sets the pace for this work, which gained instant popularity at the time of its premiere, its general categorization has been that of a "slow" movement. Whether it is or not begs more than one question and is in any case redundant. Certainly, its place in the symphonic hierarchy, along with its somber mood and change of key to the parallel minor (A minor), suggests as much. Whatever label one cares to give it, there is a great deal more than tempo that makes this Allegretto one of its composer's more astonishing creations.

The opening motive—one of only three upon which the movement relies for its shape and structure—is a simple dactyl (a long note followed by two shorter ones) spread out over eight bars (0:09). It is hardly an expansive melody, but precisely the opposite: it is in fact a single note repeated, save for the slightly migrating counterpoint provided by the bass. What's more, its voice is dark, in that Beethoven has assigned it to the violas, cellos, and basses, lending a prescient air to the proceedings.

The next eight bars propose a new phase of the melody, rather than an entirely new motive (0:25). Here the tune ambles upwards by a third, as if it were the barely conscious first uttering of a living species. A third phase, brought forth again by the violas, is really a variant that incorporates the dactyl, while also introducing a fresh melodic fragment that sets out on two half-notes (0:59). Elsewhere, the violins, towing the party line, appropriate all three phases of the dactyl motive (1:51). With the introduction of the woodwinds, trumpets, and timpani a few bars later, this overlay of material, having fully engorged itself on its various fragments, burgeons forth in a robust *fortissimo* (2:45).

While the basses pursue the dactyl below with subtle insistence, the clarinets and bassoons express a wholly new idea, one as melodious as its ambiance is hopeful (3:50). This it does in the sunnier key of A major. The first violins take second place here, assuaging the new content in a fluid stream of even-handed triplets.

The return to A minor and the original theme is precipitated by a forceful descending scale in triplets, tossed from the flutes and oboes to the violins, and finally to the cellos and basses (5:25). Though it is easy enough to make the argument that this wholly derivative material is merely transitional, it is nevertheless just as vital to the musical message as it is to the work's structural integrity. It cautions us to make no mistake as to the grim resolve with which the dactyl motive, the Allegretto's most prominent progenitor, oversees all. Transitional material, in this case, assumes a nearly programmatic posture, announcing, as it were, the return of the leader. This signals just one dimension of Beethoven's genius: to wit, an ability to invest meaning in the most unexpected places.

But here, the first and third phases of the principal melody combine in the strings and the woodwinds, enriching the texture as it engenders a certain urgency and seriousness of purpose (5:37). Here the violins and violas assume a new posture, too, taking on a jaunty if quiet sixteenth-note accompaniment in anticipation of the ensuing fugato (6:46). This timorous, if altogether too brief, fugal episode continues for some thirty-one bars, when the dactyl motive again takes over, this time announcing itself in an unabashed *fortissimo* with brassy support from the trumpets and timpani (7:45).

As if in reminiscence, the A major section and its attendant theme, proffered by the woodwinds, returns (8:08). A coda follows, in which each instrumental section is given one last opportunity to articulate the dactyl motive in a brusque dialogue of *fortissimo* and *pianissimo* exclamations (8:48).

Third movement: Presto

The capricious, even mischievous countenance of this playful Presto— a scherzo at heart, but absent the label—is an expansion of the customary and usual A–B–A structure that defines a minuet or a scherzo. While not a radical departure in formal categories, its second repetition of the trio following the return of the A section serves to intensify the work, thus satisfying its own concept.

As if to distance it entirely from the first two movements, and the "official" tonality of the symphony, Beethoven paints this scherzo in F major, but with continuous modulations into A major. The principal theme, spread out over some twenty-four bars, is a jumpy affair, the first ten measures of which disclose a rapid tumble of descending thirds entrusted to the bassoons, oboes, and violins. In a spirited response, the same instruments, with support from the basses, violas, and oboes, close the gap, as it were, modulating almost imperceptibly to A major as they ascend, with vigorously accented downbeats, to an A-natural atop the theme.

A flurry of motivic fragments ensues; contrapuntal gamesmanship is the principal capital here. The flutes and clarinets express themselves in a restless sighing motive, regularly punctuated by brief sforzando outbursts before returning to the principal theme. But it is the abrupt shift from one instrumental group to another, wherein the principal thematic material is passed so swiftly, and in fragments, between the strings and woodwinds, that imbues this scherzo with such mercurial panache.

The trio, as to be expected, is an evocation of an idyll. The key migrates to D major, while the horns mimic, in sixths and thirds, the sighing motive given to the flutes in the preceding section. The tempo is considerably more relaxed, as Beethoven indicates *Assai meno presto*. Derivative or not, the source of this theme, and what inspired Beethoven to include it, was an Austrian Pilgrim's hymn. But if Beethoven's intention was to sketch in tone the calm of the countryside, he succeeds here brilliantly. Most remarkable is the continual presence of the dominant: throughout the entire trio, the violins, followed by the trumpets, alight upon a single A-natural and hold on to it, thus prolonging musical tension.

Again, with the reader's indulgence, this is a good place to take a step back to examine yet another important dimension of musical composition. The prolongation of a single pitch is called a *pedal point*. The manner in which listeners receive this particular brand of musical event is like no other and brings us back to our earlier discussion of intonatsiia. Pedal points enhance our experience of the aforementioned synaptic connections that link one tone to another, in that they create a kind of background, or frame, against which we can more easily discern how the pitch material surrounding them, and which they modify, evolves. Indeed, the continual drone of a single pitch or pitches within the context of a busier contrapuntal fabric is not without purpose; ironically, though the prolongation of a single tone might at first appear to be a mechanism for establishing harmonic or rhythmic stability, the net effect is just the opposite: what is created is tension, uncertainty, and anxiety.

In the presence of so many motivic fragments, melodies, complex rhythms, and harmonic variants, the average listener is not necessarily aware, at least at first, of pedal points and their perpetual buzz in the musical background. But the effect is nevertheless palpable. Pedal points await resolution not only from within the music itself, but also in relation to our listening habits. Consciously or not, we expect pedal points to dissolve themselves and relieve the tension they have engendered and in which have embroiled our expectations. That they do not always do so, thus frustrating our expectations, serves only to create greater musical tension. The unruffled, even dominating presence of pedal points demands our attention, as they heighten our aural expectations in anticipation of their idiosyncratic teleology and destiny.

That said, following the return of the A section, and then, just a few bars before the movement's conclusion, a brief reiteration of the trio's horn motive, the movement comes to an abrupt halt, and resoundingly so in F major.

Fourth movement: Allegro con brio

There is a certain forthrightness about the Seventh's finale, a nearly militaristic Allegro con brio that returns us at last and in full force to A major. A four-bar introduction pits two *fortissimo* dominant chords, played by the strings, against a motivic anapest given voice by the woodwinds, trumpets, and timpani.

The principal theme, articulated with virulent confidence by the violins, is fairly rigid in its outlook. It occupies a four-bar phrase period in 2/4 time and comprises an eighth-note followed by six sixteenths punctuated by sforzandos. Only the violins are allowed access to this intense if compact thematic fragment, while the woodwinds continue to churn out the anapest that had so engaged their attention from the start. An insistent dotted figure follows, by means of which the violins (which have now coalesced around a single A-natural) turn the anapest into a blistering iamb in the blink of an eye. The same rhythmic impetus is then put to work in a new fragment, barely four bars in length before repeating, which defines itself in a consecutive series of distended minor thirds.

This closely quartered rhythmic figure is nothing if not compulsive. Its frequent repetition sports a belligerent character. What's more, there are few if any large leaps or expansive intervals to simulate vocal music; on the contrary, the pitch material tends to move almost entirely stepwise. This contributes to the musical atmosphere, which in this instance is every bit as impulsive as it is energetic. The determination of this odd, even tortured figure to so mercilessly carry itself forward, and with little variance, confounds our expectations. Elsewhere, this same motive is played out ad infinitum in the development and again in the recapitulation, where it is made subject to furious imitation (which the *New Harvard Dictionary of Music* so elegantly defines as "the statement of a single motive or melody by two of more parts or voices in succession, each part continuing as the others enter in turn") among the strings, like a dog chasing its tail. Perhaps it is no accident that the strings rule in this movement. Their unforgiving solidarity adds to the overall animus and thus to the intensity of the figure itself. Indeed, the woodwinds appropriate this tune only twice throughout, and then only briefly, as if to acknowledge its existence, but terrified to take over completely.

In the coda the music ambles fearlessly into a triple *forte*, an unusually voluminous dynamic even for Beethoven. Here, the strings roar in a series of rapid sixteenths, accompanied by the woodwinds (and timpani), which articulate double thirds on the strong beats. The ending delivers itself to our ears with inevitable presumption, bringing the Seventh Symphony to its noble conclusion.

Symphony No. 8
in F Major, Op. 93

2 Flutes, 2 Oboes, 2 Clarinets, 2 Bassoon, 2 Horns
(F, B-flat), 2 Trumpets (F), Timpani, Violins I
and II, Violas, Cellos, Basses
Composed in 1812

First performed at the Redoutensaal, Vienna,
February 27, 1814

First movement: Allegro vivace e con brio
Second movement: Allegretto scherzando
Third Movement: Tempo di menuetto
Fourth Movement: Allegro vivace

One cannot but be struck by the fact that Beethoven declined to dedicate the Eighth Symphony to anyone. For a composer to whom such tributes meant a great deal, personally and politically, could this mean that he had only himself in mind? If so, no one can deny, at the zenith of a remarkable career, that he deserved it!

On the other hand, perhaps it's no wonder. In the two years' gestation that gave birth to the Eighth Symphony, the world had become even more restless. Its passionate affair with all things libertarian had by now become jaded. Europeans, tired of years of conflict and war, were nonetheless ruled by rival political factions that were still eager to compete and control each other.

It was a period dominated by contradictions. As the Americans and British again declared war on each other, Grimm's fanciful *Fairy Tales* saw its first publication. In faraway Russia, the great Battle of Borodino, the bloodiest of all Napoleon's brutal campaigns, became legendary, so much so that decades later, Leo Tolstoi would immortalize it in *War and Peace* with prose so poignant as to rise to the level of poetry. Elsewhere, the British set Washington, D.C., on fire and Francis Scott Key penned the *Star Spangled Banner*. The year 1812 saw the births of such astute literary figures as Charles Dickens and Robert Browning, while two years later, the Marquis de Sade, the cavalier author of eighteenth-century smut, expired into his own madness.

Given those circumstances, the Eighth Symphony is a remarkable bundle of good cheer and good humor. It also signaled a gestation period for its composer, as it would be more than a decade until Beethoven until the completion of the Ninth Symphony. Of all the symphonies he had penned up until this time, Beethoven was especially fond of this one. When his puzzled protégé Carl Czerny asked him why it was that the Eighth was greeted with considerably less enthusiasm than the Seventh and was nowhere near so popular, Beethoven, who dubbed the work "my little one," is reported to have responded, "Because it's so much better!"

First movement: Allegro vivace e con brio

Two elements distinguish this jolly Allegro vivace. The first, echoing the lack of dedication, is the absence of an introduction. Not so much as a chord is offered to introduce the principal thematic material. Whether dispensing of this customary symphonic element was in itself an homage to humor is a matter of speculation, but no one ought mistake it for its composer having abandoned seriousness of purpose.

The movement sprints forward in 3/4 time, very much in the style of a minuet. The opening melody—happy, gracious, and optimistic—comprises twelve bars and is divided into three parts played *forte*, *piano*, and *forte*, respectively. Here the spirit of fraternal cooperation, hardly dead to Beethoven, is embodied by the entire orchestra, which embraces the melody and an equally lively accompaniment in the first four bars. The woodwinds command the second period of the theme, while the violins introduce the third bit to the support of the bassoons, cellos, and basses below. A new, exceptionally simple thematic fragment, evidently possessed by the subdominant pitch of B-flat, introduces itself in the first violins in the thirteenth bar, hardly an unlucky occurrence here.

A second theme, set in the remote key of D major, appears soon enough and is picked up by the violins, then echoed by the flutes, oboes, and bassoons. It is derivative of the thematic configuration of the opening four bars in that it, too, depends on a genial figure of four notes ascending in stepwise motion. A sequence of lightly nuanced arpeggios, modified by staccato, are passed among the strings in anticipation of a lovely new seven-bar theme given over wholly to the flutes and oboes and supported by a gentle undulation of eighth-notes in the violins.

The ensuing development section parts company with its composer's earlier creations, too, in that it elaborates only a single one of the exposition's themes, and that is the brief motivic material of the symphony's first few bars. This eventually culminates in a restatement of this theme in triple *forte*, which then gives way, somewhat ambiguously, to beginnings of the recapitulation. Indeed, in this instance, the recapitulation is unusually rich and fulfills much of the dramatic fervor usually reserved for the development section. Of particular note, just in advance of the coda, is a dialogue between the clarinets and the strings, which again humble the opening motivic fragment in a flurry of modulations from major to minor.

The restrained mood of this movement, while at times as bold as any of the composer's earlier creations, surrenders in large measure to the prevailing lyricism that rules it. There are remarkably few surprises, musically speaking; there are no overt statements, supported by a litany of sforzandos, to suggest anything in the least combative. The first movement of the Eighth, it seems, wants to reassure its listeners that all is well, that balance and harmony are still possible in a war-weary world, and that better days are ahead.

Second movement: Allegretto scherzando

The popular story behind this Haydnesque movement is hardly apocryphal. Beethoven was enamored of all manner of inventions, not the least of which was the metronome, a device invented by his friend Johann Mälzel. This movement, with its array of sixteenth-notes ticking away in the woodwinds, suggests something of the mechanical regularity of the metronome, and the sixteenths are imposed here to keep a watchful eye on the expressive if sauntering melody played by the violins.

This is the shortest of any movement in Beethoven's symphonic canon. Only eighty-one measures in length, the entire movement goes on for barely five minutes. The opening six bars find the violins carrying a foppish, almost indifferent melodic fragment to the accompaniment of the aforementioned sixteenths, which pipe away, in the most dulcet demeanor, in the woodwinds. There is no development section, per se, but more simply a modulation back to the original material.

The second subject, which is taken on by both first and second violins, begins with a meandering theme in *forte* followed by a series of rapid-fire sixty-fourth-notes in the even more robust dynamic of *fortissimo*. Indeed, such a furious outburst signals something of a joke in its own right, upsetting as it does the thematic status quo.

The movement ends abruptly, without warning, loudly, and in a shudder of thirty-second-notes reminiscent of Vivaldi at his most onomatopoetic.

Third movement: Tempo di menuetto

Given its overall urbanity, this comfortable throwback to an authentic minuet is no accident. It seems that Beethoven's intent, in contradiction to the scherzo whose form he at once perfected and reinvented, was to extol the older form as one whose time had not entirely expired.

The first two bars, though hardly an introduction, give impetus to the minuet proper that immediately follows. The initial upbeat gives way to no fewer than five sforzandos placed adroitly on each strong beat. The strings then articulate the ensuing principal theme, a broad affair that gives emphasis to its first downbeat, which coincidentally occurs on the highest pitch in the phrase. While the first violins sing out this hardy theme to a steady eighth-note accompaniment provided by its sister strings, a trumpet colors the proceedings with quiet assurance, which grows more pronounced at the conclusion of the A section. The bassoons find themselves especially busy in this section, entrusted with a fragment of the melody as it drifts in and out of an accompaniment figure in thirds and fifths.

The trio avails itself of a hunting call given over to the horns in customary fashion, though varied ever so pliantly moments later by a lone clarinet. Alongside this musical landscape, the cellos move things steadily along in a reliable stream of arpeggiated triplets.

Berlioz opined that this movement was essentially "ordinary," and in formal categories he was right. And yet it is exactly that devotion to the formalities of convention that is part of its charm. Here, the periodic inclusion of sforzandos is not meant as, nor ought to be interpreted as, vigorous accentuation. On the contrary, sforzandos in this case blithely underline, for the most part, the strong beats so as to lend greater clarity to the articulation. It is as if the dancer's leading foot, setting itself down firmly on the downbeat, is also reminded that movement does not just stop there, but is the catalyst that springs the body forward in tandem with his partner.

The return to the A section is uneventful, though the savvy interpreter will strive to bring attention to compositional relationships that, on the first outing, were perhaps less prominently surveyed. With regard to Furtwängler's elegant reading, listen to the subtle but perhaps slightly greater attention he pays to the bass and accompaniment figures the second time around.

Fourth movement: Allegro vivace (CD Track 8)

The motivic germ that informs the Allegro vivace, a rondo-sonata form, is extracted from the opening measures of the first movement and is at once quixotic and ethereal. A rondo-sonata combines elements of both forms, incorporating alternating recurrences of themes within the larger context of an exposition, development, and recapitulation. In this movement, for example, Beethoven revisits its few themes again and again, heightening their effect as much as their hierarchical position through unexpected modulations, imitation, and rhythmic diminution.

The violins appropriate the delicate cell of the opening, which is defined by two beats of droning triplets, followed by a sylvan figure, repeated three times, of two eighths coupled under a slur abutting a staccato quarter. Dispatched rapidly and in *pianissimo*, it is evocative of a gallop (0:00). The theme then breaks into its second period, supported by the woodwinds as it broadens into quarter-note motion and before emerging in a strident *fortissimo* (0:17).

A new, lyrical theme emerges without fanfare (0:42). The development complements itself with a frisky interplay of the strings, which focus their attention on the opening triplet and eighth-note motive, and the woodwinds, which double up in octaves and third, in quarter-note motion (1:21). Among the more salient features of this movement is the unexpected intrusion of a C-sharp in the exposition (0:16) that again forcefully raises its head, during the restatement of the principal motive in the midst of an unusually expansive coda (5:41). That the relation of this pitch is so far removed from the key of F major makes its appearance an event in its own right. What's more, it resurfaces on the heels of and in juxtaposition to a C-natural repeated in the bass, which only adds to its jarring effect.

Like a bodybuilder flexing his muscles, the last twenty-one bars alternate tonic and dominant chords on strong beats (7:16). This not only draws out the ending, but also serves to prolong our expectations of where and when the conclusion will finally occur. With these impressive *fortissimo* chords, the full complement of orchestral instruments carries the movement to its boisterous conclusion.

Symphony No. 9 in D Minor, Op. 125

Piccolo, 2 Flutes, 2 Oboes, 2 Clarinets, 2 Bassoons, Contrabassoon, 4 Horns (D, B-flat, B-flat basso, E-flat), 2 Trumpets, Alto Trombone, Tenor Trombone, Bass Trombone, Timpani, Triangle, Cymbals, Bass Drum, Violins I and II, Violas, Cellos, Basses, Soprano Solo, Alto Solo, Tenor Solo, Bass-Baritone Solo, Sopranos, Altos, Tenors, Basses

Composed 1818–24

First performed at the Kärntnertor Theater, May 7, 1824

Dedicated to Friedrich Wilhelm III of Prussia

First movement: Allegro ma non troppo, un poco maestoso

Second movement: Molto vivace; Presto

Third movement: Adagio molto e cantabile

Fourth movement: Recitative: Presto; Allegro ma non troppo; Vivace; Adagio cantabile; Allegro assai; Presto ("O Freunde"); Allegro assai ("Freude, schöner Götterfunken"); Alla marcia—Allegro assai vivace ("Froh, wie seine Sonnen"); Andante maestoso ("Seid umschlungen, Millionen!")—Adagio ma non troppo, ma divoto ("Ihr stürzt nieder"); Allegro energico, sempre ben marcato ("Freude, schöner Götterfunken—Seid umschlungen, Millionen!"); Allegro ma non tanto ("Freude, Tochter aus Elysium!"); Prestissimo ("Seid umschlungen, Millionen!")

Text of "Ode to Joy":*

German original	English translation
O Freunde, nicht diese Töne!	*Oh, friends, not these tones!*
Sondern laßt uns angenehmere	*Rather let us begin to sing*
anstimmen und freudenvollere.	*more pleasant and more joyful ones.*
Freude! Freude!	*Joy! Joy!*
Freude, schöner Götterfunken	Joy, beautiful divine spark,
Tochter aus Elysium,	maiden of Elysium,
Wir betreten feuertrunken,	we are intoxicated with fire,
Himmlische, dein Heiligtum!	heavenly being, as we enter your
Deine Zauber binden wieder	sanctuary!
Was die Mode streng geteilt;	Your spells reunite
Alle Menschen werden Brüder,	what fashion has rigidly sundered;
Wo dein sanfter Flügel weilt.	all men become brothers
	wherever your gentle wing
	reposes.
Wem der große Wurf gelungen,	Let whoever has gained the great
Eines Freundes Freund zu sein;	stake
Wer ein holdes Weib errungen,	and has become friend of a friend,
Mische seinen Jubel ein!	let whoever has won a lovely
Ja, wer auch nur eine Seele	woman,
Sein nennt auf dem Erdenrund!	add his jubilation to ours!
Und wer's nie gekonnt, der stehle	Yes, whoever in the world
Weinend sich aus diesem Bund!	merely calls a soul his own!
	And let whoever has never been
	able to do so,
	steal away in tears from this
	company.
Freude trinken alle Wesen	All beings drink joy
An den Brüsten der Natur;	at the breasts of Nature;
Alle Guten, alle Bösen	all good men, all evil men
Folgen ihrer Rosenspur.	follow her trail of roses.

* The German text was adapted by Beethoven from Friedrich Schiller's revised
(1803) version of his poem "An die Freude." (Additional text by Beethoven is in
italics.) The English translation is from Ludwig van Beethoven, *Symphonies Nos.
8 and 9 in Full Score* (New York: Dover, 1989).

Küsse gab sie uns und Reben,	She gave us kisses and the vine,
Einen Freund, geprüft im Tod;	a friend tested in death;
Wollust ward dem Wurm gegeben,	sexual pleasure was granted to the worm,
Und der Cherub steht vor Gott!	and the cherub stands in the sight of God!
Froh, wie seine Sonnen fliegen	Happily as His suns fly
Durch des Himmels prächt'gen Plan,	through heaven's splendid field,
Laufet, Brüder, eure Bahn,	run your course, brothers,
Freudig, wie ein Held zum Siegen.	joyfully as a hero to victory.
Seid umschlungen, Millionen!	Be embraced, O millions!
Diesen Kuß der ganzen Welt!	This kiss for the whole world!
Brüder, über'm Sternenzelt	Brothers! above the starry tent
Muß ein lieber Vater wohnen.	a loving Father must dwell.
Ihr stürzt nieder, Millionen?	You fall down, O millions?
Ahnest du den Schöpfer, Welt?	Do you have a presentiment of the Creator, O world?
Such' ihn über'm Sternenzelt!	Seek Him above the starry tent!
Über Sternen muß er wohnen.	Over stars He must dwell.

In the nearly two centuries since Beethoven set the first sketches for it to paper, the Ninth Symphony has transcended itself to become the apotheosis of the symphonic literature. As one of the towering achievements of Western civilization, it has been likened, significantly, to all manner of artistic and monumental achievement, from Shakespeare's *King Lear* to the Pyramids at Giza. Elsewhere, its appropriation for political propaganda, whether good or evil, and its value for commercial ends—from television news programs to popular cinema—has failed to demean either the substance or message of its immanent content.

No one, amateur or scholar, is likely to deny that the Ninth Symphony, either in spite of or because of its extraordinary complexity, stands alone as something emblematic of extramusical concerns, not the least of which are faith, humanity, conscience, power, and human potential. What's more, in appropriating the human voice for inclusion in this symphony, Beethoven legitimized, with his final stamp of approval, the very ideas, born of the French Revolution, whose time had come and gone: namely, liberty and fraternity. It is perhaps ironic that the very idea of liberty, which is nowhere explicitly extolled in the Ninth, would become, more than a century later, a substitute in Schiller's *Ode to Joy*. It did just that in 1989, when the word *Freude* ("joy") was replaced in every instance by *Freiheit* ("freedom") in Leonard Bernstein's now famous performance at the newly dismantled Berlin Wall in 1989.

In 1817, the very year that Mary Shelley's gothic novel *Frankenstein* saw its first publication, the Royal Philharmonic Society of London commissioned Beethoven to pen a new symphony. Though it was to be his ninth, its gestation period was unusually long even for a composer as prolific as he. Indeed, he had been contemplating any number of innovative ideas since the premiere, some five years earlier, of his Eighth Symphony. The notion of setting to music an abbreviated segment of Schiller's popular *Ode to Joy* had been on his mind since his youth; he had sketched out and set it to music as early as 1793.

It was a fruitful period politically, as well. The Napoleonic Wars had at long last ended in 1815. Beethoven, who once valued as a hero the man in whose name they were fought, had long since dismissed him for the tyrant he turned out to be. While there was hardly a moratorium on international conflicts in consequence of the cessation of hostilities in Europe, Napoleon's fading into history, as well as his forced exile, signaled the end of an era. That alone likely proved an inspiration to the now mature Beethoven as he set out to write his magnum opus.

Certainly, it was his most ambitious work and, at just under an hour in performance, his longest. At the premiere in 1824, Beethoven, by then completely deaf, declined to sit in the wings or in the audience. Instead, he shared the stage, "co-conducting," as it were, with the theater's music director, Michael Umlauf, who had instructed all in attendance to ignore the composer's gestures.

Even at that late stage, Beethoven called for doubling the wood-winds. The sheer volume of participants in this symphony was in itself a reflection of its largesse as much as its purpose, which was as much musical as it was humanistic. Indeed, only a year later, Ferdinand Ries enlarged the orchestra and chorus yet again to include some four hundred players and singers.

The public reception at the premiere, which was not to be duplicated a few weeks later at its second performance, was so enthusiastic that a military squadron was called in to keep the peace.

First movement: Allegro ma non troppo, un poco maestoso

Nothing could be more remarkable or ingenious than the opening of this first movement, which inspired so many composers, including Wagner. Emerging from a collection of open fifths played *pianissimo* by the strings, as if the orchestra were merely tuning up, the symphony begins its journey. The horns, which sustain an open fifth, as well, project themselves over the strings in a quiet yet sonorous background halo. The overall effect is that of dawn becoming day, or of a vague reverie slowly but deliberately taking shape and coming to life, which it does indeed only moments later.

Seventeen bars into the movement, the entire orchestra, now in unison and in a confident *fortissimo*, ushers in the principal theme in D minor, which comprises only four bars. Its rhythm is iambic as it follows its downward trajectory in thirds.

The musical atmosphere remains, on the whole, curiously restrained. The iambic motive that informs the opening remains for the most part the driving force throughout the movement. In spite of the music's sometimes combative character, the instrumental textures remain largely transparent, with the strings given over largely to the iambic motive while the trumpets and woodwinds share in supportive roles. The flutes and clarinets accede, however, to a more prominent role in the recapitulation, taking on the likewise fragmentary motives, not one of them rising to the level of a full-fledged theme, which Beethoven draws so skillfully in the exposition. Meanwhile the strings and woodwinds, making no pretense of a descending eighth-note fragment that precipitates things to come, roll alongside the ever-present timpani, bouncing these ideas off one another.

The inclusion of four horns—the first time Beethoven had seen fit to do so in any of his symphonies—lends a certain nobility to the proceedings, though perhaps nowhere more than in the drawn-out coda. The initial subject in unisons that presided so mightily over the movement's murky beginning makes a return in the recapitulation, but now with greater optimism and in D major. Here the trembling timpani assume an air that is more victorious than prescient, while the trumpets blare out the iambic motive with increasing fervor. As the movement draws to an end, the horns are heard, in the major, in the distance, while the woodwinds, led by the oboes, emerge with a tremulous, even disturbing variant of the iambic motive, now modified with trills, that accumulates energy and brings the movement to its decisive end.

Second movement: Molto vivace (CD Track 9)

Here Beethoven throws a wrench into the symphonic status quo. For the first time in his symphonic canon, a scherzo is positioned between the first and slow movements. What's more, this particular scherzo makes an auspicious debut; it starts out as a five-voice fugue, thus cleverly combing two forms.

The principal theme is a puckish train of rising staccato quarter-notes in stepwise motion (0:06). The strings, in the role of a musical pied piper, lead the way as their instrumental colleagues follow. This gradual marshaling of orchestral mass culminates in *fortissimo*, before moving on to the second part of the material, now in E minor. While up to this point the phrasing has been periodic, that is, organized in consistent units of three or four bars at a time, Beethoven suddenly indicates the rhythm is to be taken at one beat for every three bars, then four bars (*ritmo di tre battute, ritmo di quattro battute*), thus creating subtle shifts of accentuation, especially on the downbeats (2:49; 2:57).

The coloration is likewise ingenious, as the overall texture remains essentially transparent. The supportive interruptions of the timpani, combined with the playful extensions of the woodwinds, are likewise used to remarkable effect. A brief accelerando anticipates the ensuing trio, which emerges in the parallel major key of D, though now in duple (alla breve) time (4:51). Even in this late work, Beethoven, as always respectful of tradition, offers yet another woodsy, bucolic melody at first taken on by the oboes and clarinets, then followed by the horns. Yet even here he is aware of the damaging potential of monotony; the second part of the theme, a rising-scale passage that commences on the tonic, is given to the violas and cellos as if to make certain that nothing of the kind could possibly occur (5:05). Soon enough, after the horns and oboes regurgitate the trio's principal themes, the strings once again take the lead. With the return of the A section (8:11), its major motives now dynamically intensified, this last of Beethoven's symphonic scherzos comes to an end— in duple time!

Indeed, the fact that this is the last of Beethoven's orchestral excursions into the scherzo brings us to yet one more, rather philosophical, dimension of intonatsiia. While neither the composer himself nor the public could have known that he would be dead only three years following the premiere of the Ninth Symphony, today listeners judge from a historically informed perspective. In the first chapters, I opined that intonatsiia concerns itself as much with the tension between notes and phrases as it does with tension between whole movements. On a larger scale, it also addresses issues of place and time; there is something enormously touching and perhaps significant about the last of a composer's works. Today we have the advantage of being able to consider Beethoven's symphonies, and the various forms they engage, side by side, as it were. In so doing we can also determine the extent of his artistic and intellectual development, as if we were watching a child grow from a boy to a man. While that may not tell us much if anything specific about the music itself, it does reveal much about his approach to both compositional strategy and aesthetic philosophy.

This is what the Russian semiologist and philosopher Mikhail Bakhtin once described as "great time," a concept that I referred to earlier and that now deserves its author's elaboration:

> Yet the artwork extends its roots into the distant past. . . . Trying to understand terms of the conditions of its most immediate time, will never enable us to penetrate into its semantic depths. Enclosure within the epoch also makes it impossible to understand the work's future life in subsequent centuries, this life appears

as a kind of paradox. Works break through the boundaries of their own time, they live in centuries, that is, in great time, and frequently (with great works, always), their lives there are more intense and fuller than are their lives within their own time . . . it is frequently the case, however, that a work gains in significance, that is, it enters *great time*.

But the work cannot live in future centuries without having somehow absorbed past centuries as well. If it had belonged entirely to today (that is, were a product of its own time) and not a continuation of the past or essentially related to the past, it could not live in the future. Everything that belongs to the present dies along with the present. . . . It seems paradoxical that . . . great works continue to live in the distant future. In the process of their posthumous life they are enriched with new meaning, new significance: it is as though these works outgrew what they were in the epoch of their creation.

Third movement: Adagio, molto cantabile

The principal theme of this endearing slow movement, given over wholly to the first violins, follows an abbreviated two-bar introduction played by the oboes and bassoons. The rhythmic pace, though excruciatingly slow, engages our attention for its underlying intensity and even vivacity. It is for this reason that this Adagio, cast in the comforting key of B-flat major, presents considerable difficulties for conductors, particularly in the realm of intonatsiia; what occupies the languorous, even timeless pace that informs so much of it demands both the evocation and material realization of musical intensity.

The theme itself proceeds mostly in stepwise motion, with a single leap of a perfect fifth lending expressive capital to its otherwise ardent demeanor. The tempo picks up a bit only twenty-five bars later, where Beethoven indicates a change to Andante moderato and moves things forward with a new theme in D major. The time signature changes, too, from 4/4 to 3/4. Here again the violins and violas assume the bulk of responsibility before things return to the original, slower tempo some eighteen bars later.

This tender second theme, like the first, relies on stepwise motion as the measure of its expressive personality. It is a four-bar phrase, played in unison by the second violins and violas, that angles upward with somewhat timorous determination, as if to make itself known. A return to B-flat major augurs the set of variations that follows. In the midst of all this, the second theme (andante moderato) makes its return in G major, this time carried forth by the woodwinds, with the oboes taking the lead, a lead that they maintain when the principal theme, too, returns some eighteen bars later.

The violins proceed with the appropriate wanderlust of their original theme, now elaborated in a steady stream of triplets and dulcetly accompanied by the woodwinds. An unexpected salvo of the horns and trumpets—two short sixteenth-note bursts followed by an eighth—briefly interrupts the lyrical profusion, and does so once more following the next entry of the violins. The movement ends just as peacefully as it began, but with all the orchestral instruments now coming together as one, as if in expression of their solidarity.

Fourth movement

The sheer immensity of this, the final movement of Beethoven's symphonic canon, is daunting enough for any analysis. Nor does it help, given its fantastic breadth and humanity, that words cannot possibly express, metaphorically or otherwise, so much as an iota of its meaning. That said, let's have a look at how this gargantuan structure, which is nothing if not an expression of collective ecstasy, works on its own terms.

Though one of the longest single movements Beethoven ever wrote, this one is actually a model of economy. That is largely because it amounts in fact to four distinct movements within a movement, or, to cite Charles Rosen, a "symphony within a symphony."

The opening is a model of compositional deception. In this first "sub-movement," things begin vigorously enough with a loud announcement, by the trumpets, horns, woodwinds, and timpani, of an impressive but defiant theme. This seven-bar passage exploits pitch repetition and dissonance to make its point, and in startling contrast to what follows. Indeed, just as we wonder if this initial theme has had its say, the cellos, now segregated, make their move, giving voice to a theme that will eventually become the setting for "O Freunde," or "O friends."

Perhaps in a bid to express his dissatisfaction with the goings-on, or as a means to contradict them, Beethoven then takes us back to the themes of the earlier movements. We hear first the open fifths that gave birth to the first movement, then the mischievous staccato of the Scherzo, and finally the conciliatory beginnings of the slow movement.

This brings us to consider yet another extraordinary facet of Beethoven's genius. In his late works especially, the introduction of the thematic material used in an earlier part of the composition becomes a compositional technique as well as an aesthetic principle in its own right. Reminiscence, no longer simply an extramusical idea or the evocation of a memory, now rises to the level of an art form. Though the expression of a sentiment, musical reminiscence, at least in this composer's vision, bears nothing in common with sentimentality. In Beethoven's hands, and in so many of his mature works, such repetition is neither saccharine nor gratuitous. On the contrary, where earlier themes reappear and circulate in new contexts, it is more than an occasion for reflection and contemplation. It is as if the music, cognizant of its own power and humanity, asks us take a look back on our own thoughts and memories as a means to contemplate the meaning of our lives.

The initial participation of these now familiar themes is no accident. Though Beethoven may indeed have wanted us to reconsider their function in their musical hierarchy, it is his ultimate rejection of them that lends significance to the new theme, arguably the most famous in the history of Western music that emerges just after. It is the theme of joy ("Freude, schöner Götterfunken") that will be later be intoned by the chorus. In a passage marked *Allegro assai*, the cellos introduce this most optimistic tune, only to be joined in unison a few bars later by the violas. The bassoons, wasting no time in making themselves known, jump in with their own contrapuntal response. A burgeoning crescendo, rising to *forte*, gives way to the re-presentation of the joy theme in the full orchestra, its horns and trumpets ablaze.

The woodwinds take charge of an anxious transitional passage that follows, while the violins and violas run furiously ahead in a persistent torrent of sixteenth-notes. A timorous new thematic fragment peers out from the flutes in *subito piano*, before both the key and time signature return to D minor and 3/4, respectively. Here, the gripping dissonances of the beginning, recaptured and poised yet again against the portentous thundering of the timpani, are now contradicted by a solo baritone to whom Schiller's persuasive edict "O Freunde, nicht diese Töne!" ("O friends, not these tones!") is entrusted.

The boisterous *Allegro* that follows again engages the baritone, first as soloist and then as a member of the vocal quartet, as well as the full chorus, who at last intone Schiller's famous words "Freude, schöner Götterfunken, Tochter aus Elysium" ("Joy, beautiful divine spark, Daughter of Elysium"). Accompanied by the woodwinds, trumpets, and particularly prominent timpani, the singers find their energy level emboldened; they certainly have their work cut out for them if they are going to be heard above the general din. What's more, the specificity of the articulation, which throws slurs over each eighth-note couplet, serves to enrich and intensify the contrapuntal texture.

The Alla marcia forms an entirely new section, or second "movement." Marked *Allegro assai vivace*, it announces itself in B-flat major and commences in the sprightly time signature of 6/8. The bassoons blurt out six single B-flats, separated from each other by rests, on off-beats. This Alla marcia tips its symphonic hat to a marching band, including as it does cymbals, a triangle, a piccolo, and a bass drum.

The music is set in the so-called Turkish style, which was hardly music of such exotic origins, but rather a compositional strategy that gained enormous popularity in the classical era; witness the last movement "Alla Turca" of Mozart's A Major Piano Sonata. What the style did bear in common with the music of Istanbul was the instrumentation: in the marching band music of Turkey the use of the triangle, cymbals, and bass drum was conventional.

At this point a tenor soloist enters the fray and, like a peacock proudly showing off his feathers, advances a new theme set to another of Schiller's verses "Froh, wie seine Sonnen fliegen, Durch des Himmels prächt'gen Plan" ("Happily as His suns fly through heaven's splendid field"). Echoing these words, the full chorus joins in with even greater gusto. The orchestra ensues with an energetic double fugue before the chorus again imposes itself.

A somber Andante maestoso forms the next "movement" to gain the upper hand as the chorus, beginning with the basses and tenors, sings Schiller's verse "Seid umschlungen, Millionen!" ("Be embraced, O millions!"). No fewer than three trombones lend their support. A stirring *Adagio ma non troppo, ma divoto* throws the chorus and orchestra into nearly religious fervor while the chorus intones, "Ihr stürzt nieder, Millionen?" ("You fall down, O millions?"). Indeed, a moment of the most ethereal dimensions brings this Adagio to a close: as the woodwinds hover steadily on a double thirds, the chorus, availing itself of an unusually high tessitura, sings, "Über Sternen muss er wohnen" ("Beyond the stars must he dwell").

Suddenly, the tempo changes, as does the key. Beethoven returns us to D major in an inspired finale, or fourth "movement," dubbed *Allegro energico, sempre ben marcato*. The chorus is heard again in "Freude, schöner Götterfunken," this time in a rousing fugato with the orchestra.

The quartet of vocal soloists, in tandem with the chorus, joins forces to extol the exalted sentiments, first in "Freude, Tochter aus Elysium" and then in "Alle Menschen werden Brüder!" ("All men will be brothers"). The vocal quartet, with the thinnest instrumental accompaniment and harnessing the tempo to a *Poco adagio*, returns to prominence in an unusually elaborate survey of this same verse. Indeed, the soprano soloist is enjoined to sing an impossibly high B, a feat that bears witness to the old story that Beethoven, interested only in musical values, was ruthless with regard to the needs and limitations of singers.

To say that the final minutes of this great symphony, brought to its thrilling close by its instrumentalists and singers in a furious *prestissimo*, give one goose bumps is an understatement. The immense, uncompromising finality of it all is eerie, even mystical, as if Beethoven knew this work was to be his ultimate farewell.

And with that, the body of Beethoven's symphonic output, which remains among the greatest achievements in the history of civilization, comes to a close, though not to an end. On the contrary, as generations to come have yet to discover these magnificent works, we can say with confidence that it is only the beginning.

Glossary

accelerando A gradual heightening or cumulative quickening of tempo.

adagio A slow tempo, but neither turgid nor comatose. An adagio must move, broadly.

affect Comes from the *Affektenlehre*, or "Doctrine of Affects," a seventeenth-century aesthetic ideology holding that the emotions could be codified in sound and that a rhetorical grammar of such affections could be made part of compositional procedure. Though not exactly interchangeable in our use of the terms, it is a species of *inflection* and is best described as referring to the degree of emphasis, dynamic weight, or perspective performers invest in any given motivic figuration.

allegretto A lively, quick, and above all playful tempo, but not quite so fast as allegro.

allegro Generally understood to be a fast or moderately fast tempo, but in music of the baroque and classical eras, especially, it refers to character and disposition; it can be construed to mean "cheerful" or "happy."

andante A gracious walking tempo, not too slow nor too quick. Subject to any number of gradations.

articulation The manner in which a performer distinguishes, by means of attack, prolongation, and release, certain tones, motives, phrases, and groups of pitches individually and in relation to each other. Composers either spell out or provide symbols to indicate types of articulation, such as staccato, legato, wedges, tenuto, and other accent marks.

baroque music Music composed roughly between 1590 and 1750 and that embraces certain styles and techniques attributable to the aesthetic ideas, formulations, and philosophy of the era. Because of its long run, it is usually divided into three distinct subperiods, each governed by specific innovations. Opera, the fugue, and the harmonization of a ground bass were products of baroque invention.

cadence That which harmonically demarcates and provides a sense of resolution, with varying degrees of finality, the end of a phrase or larger section of a work. In its harmonic tendency to move back toward the key of the work, cadence is also an expression of a composition's tonality.

cadenza An extended solo passage usually, but not only, found in a concerto. It typically comes toward the end of a concerto or sonata form movement, before the coda, and it elaborates and ornaments the principal themes of the work with a view toward showing off the skill of its composer or soloist, or both. Though composers sometimes write out the cadenza, performers, too, occasionally write their own.

canon A musical pattern defined by a thematic subject that is presented, then successively imitated by one or more voices commencing on different pitches. There are different kinds of canon: fixed, which is imitation by rote, and free, which introduces modifications of pitch material and rhythm.

classical era The period of musical composition that extended from the early eighteenth through the early nineteenth centuries. Its exact division into years is difficult to measure, as classicism evolved slowly and its attendant techniques and aesthetics eventually bled into romanticism. Characteristics of music of the classical era include periodic phrasing; longer harmonic rhythms; a prevalence of simpler, more natural melodic designs; homophonic textures; and greater use of specifically marked dynamic contrasts.

coda　　　　　The concluding section of a movement or single composition that usually encapsulates the work's principal themes. A coda may be as brief as a few measures, or elaborate and extensive.

counterpoint　　The simultaneous unfolding of two or more melodies, and the various compositional principles that govern their existence and formulation—that is, their movement apart or away from each other, their rhythmic differences, and the resultant harmonies they create in relation to each other.

crescendo,　　A gradual, cumulative increase or decrease in vol-
decrescendo　ume indicated by hairpin signs or written out as a word by the composer. This intensification of sound in either direction informs the affective character of the passage it modifies.

development　　The middle section of a movement in sonata form wherein the principal themes and motivic ideas are varied, elaborated, intensified, ornamented, en route to the recapitulation.

dominant　　　Every major and minor scale consists of seven pitches; the fifth degree scale is called the *dominant*. A chord constructed around this pitch includes the seventh degree of the scale. The tendency of the seventh degree to move toward its neighboring

	tonic pitch is strong and creates in listeners a feeling of strong expectation and desire for resolution.
dotted notes	A dot placed just alongside a pitch increases the temporal value of that note by one half of its original value. Two dots set in this way increase the value by yet another quarter of that value.
exposition	The first section of a sonata, in which the principal themes of the composition are presented in juxtaposition one to the other, and which includes at least one major modulation to a secondary key, most often, but not necessarily, the dominant.
fermata	A half-moon-shaped symbol turned on its side (⌢) and set over a rest or note to indicate prolongation.
forte; fortissimo	Loud; very loud (though best interpreted as "strong; very strong").
fugue	A composition in which a theme (also known as a *subject*) is stated and then repeated consecutively in two or more voices in imitative counterpoint. This confluence of voices is then elaborated, extended, varied, modulated, developed in any number of ways.
fugato	A usually brief contrapuntal section that occurs within a sonata movement or other form and that does not develop into a full-blown fugue, although it is at once contrapuntal and imitative (the essential characteristics of a fugue).
hemiola	A kind of rhythmic substitute, wherein two measures in triple meter are both notated and played as if they were three bars in duple meter.
intonatsiia	A Russian concept that defines intervallic relationships, referring to and codifying the implicit musical tension, both rhythmic and dynamic, that we experience *between* any two pitches in a motive or

melody. On a larger scale, it also governs transitions that link larger phrase units. Intonatsiia is the musical equivalent of a neuron, functioning as a conduit that carries musically relevant information such as rhythm, nuance, and dynamic tendencies from one pitch to another.

larghetto   Not quite so slow as largo.

lento   Slow.

menuetto (minuet)   An elegant dance in 3/4 time that had its origins in seventeenth-century France. It is usually in two-part (binary) form, and its second beats are often accented. When danced, the minuet was a little slower than when performed strictly as instrumental music.

microdynamics   On the order of an inflection; the slight fluctuation of dynamics within the smallest possible motivic or phrase unit.

motive, motif   A brief rhythmic unit of a specific duration and design that acquires its own identity and becomes the basis of more elaborate structures, movements, and whole works.

ostinato   A repetitive rhythmic and melodic pattern reiterated over the course of a composition, usually carried in the bass.

pedal point   A single tone, reiterated and sustained under changing harmonic patterns and over an extended period. While pedal points frequently occur in the bass, they can also be dispatched in any voice to enhance harmonic and rhythmic tension.

piano; pianissimo   Soft; very soft.

pizzicato   For stringed instruments, an articulation wherein the string is plucked with the fingers rather than bowed.

polyphony	Wherein several musical voices, or lines, are heard in combination, and where each line has an independent character.
presto; prestissimo	Very fast; faster still than presto.
recapitulation	In sonata form, the concluding section of a movement, wherein all the principal themes of the work are restated, usually in the tonic key.
rallentando	Increasingly slow.
ritardando	Slowing down.
rondo	A form in several sections, wherein the principal section (A) alternates with subsequent sections (B, C, D, etc.). Whenever the principal (A) section is restated, it is usually in the tonic key.
scherzo	A light, playful, even mischievous dance form that in the late eighteenth and nineteenth centuries often replaced the minuet as a movement in symphonies and in instrumental music. It is played swiftly in 3/4 time and includes a contrasting trio section.
sforzando	A sudden, interruptive accentuation.
sonata form	The traditional form used most often in first movements of instrumental music from the classical period and beyond. Though it can be identified by a few standard organizational procedures exposition, development, and recapitulation, as well as key relationships that juxtapose tonic and dominant in the first section, and so on it is best viewed as a dynamic process.
staccato	The distinct separation of a pitch from its neighboring notes. From the baroque era onward, staccato was an articulation marking, indicated by a dot above the note that instructed the player to cancel the prevailing legato.

tempo	The rate of speed at which a piece of music is played; a specific tempo is indicated by the composer, who relies on a performer to respect his instructions according to the universally understood precepts and in accordance with contemporary performance practice.
tonality	The organization of tones around a single central pitch, or tonic. Tonality comprises all twelve major and minor keys, as well as the scales, triads, and harmonic functions that define them.
tremolo	The rapid repetition of a single pitch or chord. Used for purposes of affective and dramatic intensification.
triplet	Three notes of equal value played in place of two notes of equal value.

Selected Bibliography

Adorno, Theodor W. *Introduction to the Sociology of Music*. Translated by E. B. Ashton. New York: Continuum International, 1976.

Bakhtin, Mikhail. "Response to a Question from the *Novy Mir* Editorial Staff." In *Speech Genres and Other Late Essays*, edited by Caryl Emerson and Michael Holquist, translated by Vern W. McGee, 1–9. Austin: University of Texas Press, 1986.

Beethoven, Ludwig Van. *Beethoven's Letters: With Explanatory Notes by Dr. A. C. Kalischer*. New York: Dover, 1972.

————. *Symphonies Nos. 1–9 in Full Score*. 3 vols. New York: Dover, 1989.

Berlioz, Hector. *Beethoven by Berlioz*. Compiled and translated by Ralph De Sola. Boston: Crescendo, 1975.

Bernstein, Leonard. *The Joy of Music*. Pompton Plains, N.J.: Amadeus Press, 2004.

Blaukopf, Kurt. *Musical Life in a Changing Society: Aspects of music sociology*. Translated by David Marinelli. Portland, Ore.: Amadeus Press, 1982.

Bonds, Mark Evan. *Music as Thought: Listening to the Symphony in the Age of Beethoven*. Princeton, N.J.: Princeton University Press, 2006.

Brown, Clive. *Classical and Romantic Performing Practice, 1750–1900*. New York: Oxford University Press, 1997.

Burk, John. *The Life and Works of Beethoven*. New York: The Modern Library, 1946.

Burnham, Scott, and Michael P. Steinberg, eds. *Beethoven and His World*. Princeton, N.J.: Princeton University Press, 2000.

Harnoncourt, Nikolaus. *The Musical Dialogue: Thoughts on Monteverdi, Bach, and Mozart*. Portland, Ore.: Amadeus Press, 1984.

Jankélévitch, Vladimir. *Music and the Ineffable*. Translated by Carolyn Abbate. Princeton, N.J.: Princeton University Press, 1983.

Lang, Paul Henry. *Music in Western Civilization*. New York: Norton, 1997.

The New Harvard Dictionary of Music. Edited by Don Michael Randel. Cambridge, Mass.: Harvard University Press, 1986.

Painter, Karen. *Symphonic Aspirations: German Music and Politics, 1900–1945*. Cambridge, Mass: Harvard University Press, 2007.

Rosen, Charles. *Critical Entertainments: Music Old and New*. Cambridge, Mass.: Harvard University Press, 2000.

————. *The Romantic Generation*. Cambridge, Mass.: Harvard University Press, 1995.

Weingartner, Felix. *On the Performance of Beethoven's Symphonies and Other Essays*. New York: Dover, 1969.

CD Track Listing

All performances on the enclosed CD were conducted by Wilhelm Furtwängler.

1. Symphony No. 1: Menuetto; Allegro molto e vivace (Third movement) (3:50)
   Berlin Philharmonic, September 19, 1954
   From Music & Arts CD 792

2. Symphony No. 2: Scherzo: Allegro (Third movement) (4:06)
   Vienna Philharmonic Orchestra, October 1, 1948
   From Music & Arts CD 942

3. Symphony No. 3: Allegro con brio (First movement) (16:41)
   Berlin Philharmonic, December 8, 1952
   From Music & Arts CD 869

4. Symphony No. 4: Adagio (Second movement) (11:47)
   Vienna Philharmonic, September 4, 1953
   From Music & Arts CD 792

5. Symphony No. 5: Allegro con brio (First movement) (8:10)
   Berlin Philharmonic Orchestra, May 25, 1947
   From Music & Arts CD 789

6. Symphony No. 6: Thunderstorm: Allegro (Fourth movement) (4:20)
   Berlin Philharmonic Orchestra, May 25, 1947
   From Music & Arts CD 789

7. Symphony No. 7: Allegretto (Second movement) (10:25)
   Stockholm Philharmonic, November 12–13, 1948
   From Music & Arts CD 793

8. Symphony No. 8: Allegro vivace (Fourth movement) (7:42)
   Stockholm Philharmonic, November 12–13, 1948
   From Music & Arts CD 793

9. Symphony No. 9: Scherzo (Second movement) (12:00)
   Philharmonia Orchestra, Lucerne Festival, August 22, 1954
   From Music & Arts CD 790

Courtesy of Music & Arts.
℗ 2008 Music & Arts Programs of America, Inc.